DRINKING

&

KNOWING THINGS

MICHAEL AMON

Book Designed by Acepub

INTRODUCTION

Some people are obsessively into wine. Like Tyrion Lannister. Or that one friend of yours who tells everyone he's a "wine guy".

These bush league players got nothing on me. I take wine obsession to extreme levels. Besides traveling to every major wine region in the world, and studying wine for years and achieving a number of advanced wine certifications, and writing a handful of books about wine, I also started the entire wine industry in the Kingdom of Bhutan in the Himalayas, just because I thought it would be cool if they made wine there.

Anyway, my friends had been after me for years to give them wine recommendations. After years of urging, I finally started up a weekly wine recommendation that I sent out to them. This is what morphed into the wine master class you are about to embark upon.

How to Use This Book:

Up to you, really. You can read it straight through cover to cover, and you will learn some things. And probably laugh your ass off along the way. That said, I firmly believe that wine is a personal journey that must be experienced rather than simply read about.

Consequently, I would recommend that you use this book as follows: There are fifty-two wine recommendations in here. Get a significant other, or a friend, or even your douchey next-door neighbor that you don't really like, but have to get along with because your kids are friends, or repurpose your Wednesday night book club from talking about Oprah's stupid latest selection to learning cool shit and drinking some kickass wine. Doesn't matter – find someone or someones who are interested enough in learning about wine that they will go on the journey with you. They don't have to have any knowledge of wine, only an interest in it and a desire to learn more.

Every week read one of the recommendations, which will take you like ten minutes, and order a bottle of that wine. I've put recommendations for specific bottles into the book to make it easy for you. Drink the bottle with your partner-in-wine and see what you think about it.

I guarantee that if you do this, after three months you'll start to feel much more comfortable about wine. Within six months, you will be more knowledgeable about wine than anyone you know, and will likely become the de facto sommelier of your social circle. At the end of the year, you'll be able to go toe-to-toe with any sommelier or wine expert. And you'll have fun doing it.

But you'll need to be open minded and willing to get outside your comfort zone.

Drinking and Knowing Things Principles:

1. I am all about value. I'd rather drink a $25 bottle of kickass wine that no one has ever heard of than spend $150 on a bottle of another stereotypical overoaked indistinguishable Napa Cab. The wines in here on average should be no more than about $25. So your masterclass in wine is gonna cost you roughly $1250 in wine for the entire year (plus shipping if you order online). For some of the recommendations you may have to spend a bit more, just by virtue of what kind of wine it is, but for others they'll be much cheaper.

2. I believe all wine has some sort of purpose to it. Huge voluptuous reds, austere acidic whites, fortified wines, super sweet, sparkling, orange, pink, you name it. They all have some reason for existing. My motive is to figure out how and when to drink certain wines. Port makes a shitty breakfast wine, but a Jurançon with bacon and eggs is ridiculously good. If I can figure out why certain wines exist, I can figure out how to drink them. So be prepared for recommendations on not only what to drink but how and when to drink them.

3. If you say you only drink "xxxx" (insert red, white, Chardonnay, wines from California, whatever here) then you are an asshole. It's totally fine to like whatever it is that you like, but when you become dogmatic about it, you are limiting your ability to truly experience and understand wine. If you're That Guy, you're probably not gonna like this masterclass. You should opt out now.

4. You are NOT going to like everything in here. That's totally fine. You can't begin to imagine how much shitty wine I had to drink in order to figure out what I like and don't like. These recommendations are what I think are awesome. Your journey will be different. The goal of this is to figure out what is right for you, in an entertaining manner. And by entertaining, I mean drinking.

    I get asked a lot about what a "good" wine is. I have lots of opinions on this, but the best definition I have ever heard was from Paul Grieco, who was one of the founders of one of the most cool and irreverent wine bars ever – Terroir in New York. His definition (which I'm sure I'm misquoting) is "A good wine is one where you take a sip and it makes you want to take another sip. Then you take another sip and it makes you want to finish the glass. Then when you finish the glass you want to have another glass."

    That's it in a nutshell. There doesn't need to be any mystique to it. Do you want to have another sip?

    My hope for you is that for many of these wines, you want to take another sip.

5. Wherever you live, you are going to be limited in sourcing some of these recommendations by what's available to you. Especially if you live in America where our draconian three-tier wine distribution laws are holdovers from Prohibition and religious zealotry and greed. (Did you know that before we had income taxes our government was fully funded on taxes from alcohol sales? True story.) Point is that depending on where you live it may be hard to come by some of these and direct shipping could be forbidden. If you live in one of these states (e.g. Pennsylvania or Texas or Utah or...), my suggestion is to find a small local wine shop and let them know what you are doing and have them source these recommendations for you. They'll probably be super stoked that someone is interested in wine, and helping you will give them a well-needed respite from hawking another bottle of buttery California Chardonnay.

6. I thought long and hard about how to put links in here to recommend specific bottles. This is way harder than you might think because

inventories get depleted. Web sites change. I'm sure that the moment I put out this book at least one of these links is already obsolete. I've come up with the following approach - I am going to recommend a specific bottle from a specific producer. For those of you reading this book in electronic format, I'll make that a hyperlink to that bottle on www.wine-searcher.com. For those of you reading this in print format you will need to either open Google and type that bottle in (I know, hard work) or I would recommend that you go to www.wine-searcher.com and type the bottle in directly there.

I elected to use this approach, not necessarily because I think Wine Searcher is the best or only method of tracking down wines, but they do a pretty good job of showing who sells a specific bottle of wine in your country and/or zip code or online. Also, you can filter by who has the lowest price (bonus!). It's an imperfect solution, but the best I could come up with. If that doesn't work, get a little creative. You can always try Googling a little, or talk to your local wine store clerk and see what other similar options are available to you.

Also, working a bit to track down a certain wine makes it fun. It's like a scavenger hunt. With a buzz for a prize at the end.

7. I am not affiliated in any way with Wine Searcher or any of the wineries or wines I recommend here (or with Google, more's the pity). I get no financial incentives for recommending specific wines. I have no skin in this game other than to do cool shit with wine.

If you're still reading and ready to change your life then buckle the fuck up because shit's about to get real.

CONTENTS

Drinking & Knowing Things

#1: NEBBIOLO

"Oh, you're a wine guy? What's your favorite wine?"

I hate that fucking question. First Pro Tip: Don't ask that fucking question.

The main reason I hate it is because I find it unanswerable. What am I doing? When and where am I doing it? Is there food involved? Each producer and vintage can be different. How precise do I need to be with this answer?

It's like music. Raining Blood by Slayer is an awesome song to do heavy squats to, but it is a poor accompaniment to a romantic interlude, and it is non-functional for supporting guided meditations. Wine, like music, depends on the circumstances. (Wikipedia: please take note of the first ever Slayer reference in a wine recommendation.)

When asked, I usually gloss over that question, or simply respond Burgundy and move on. However, if pressed, rather than a specific wine, I can think about grapes or regions that I am very fond of for certain reasons. Nebbiolo falls into that category. I love Nebbiolo. It's fantastic on its own, and it pairs ridiculously well with food.

Flavor-wise, the standard descriptors are tar and rosés. Which I somewhat agree with. I also tend to get floral notes, truffles and often a whiff of licorice. Both tannins and acid are high, which makes it the perfect wine to drink with a super fatty ribeye (ditch those young oaky Napa cabs, people...).

Now, there is only one place to get Nebbiolo, and that is Northern Italy, Piedmont to be specific. This is where my friend Mina will raise her hand and remind me that Luke Lambert is making Nebbiolo in Yarra

Valley, Australia. I will respond by informing her that the only reason she brings that up is because she thinks Luke is a total smokeshow, and will take any opportunity to talk about him. I have great respect for Luke and am optimistic he may be able to come up with some great shit from down there, but it is going to take him at least a decade to dial it in, and another five years to age it.

I don't have that kind of time. Daddy thirsty....

Anyway, in Piedmont there are a ton of small towns and communes that produce Nebbiolo. You are likely familiar with the wines of Barolo and Barbaresco. Both are Nebbiolo, both are great, and both are expensive. I have some pointed opinions of what's going down in those regions right now, but I will save those. We're gonna talk about some other places.

First, recognize that Nebbiolo is the most commonly used name in Piedmont for this grape. But in true Italian fashion they use a bunch of other names for it, including Spanna, Chiavannasca, and Picutener. (Note that Piedmont is about the size of Massachusetts. So we need seventeen different names for things.) Moreover, each town or commune is going to label their wine by the name of that town. And the label could be in Italian. You could theoretically see a bottle of wine made from the Nebbiolo grape, which would not contain the word Nebbiolo anywhere on the label or in any of the descriptors.

These are the wines we want! These are the ones that can be ridiculously awesome, and will be super inexpensive. At least until people figure out that they can drive eight miles north of Barolo and buy a super great bottle of Nebbiolo for $10. And then the demand curve shifts out, a new equilibrium is established at a higher price point, and then...

Fuck, sorry. Was having Econ grad school flashbacks for a moment there. Anyway, the point is that at one time Barolo was super cheap, until people figured out how great it is. Now it's not. We're looking for the next Barolo that no one knows.

Some Dope Nebbiolo Choices:

I hesitated to even put this first one out there, because it is awesome and also super small so if all of you go nuts buying this it may become harder for me to get. So just read about it. Don't actually buy any.

The region is called Valtellina, and the wines will be labelled as such. It is all the way to the North, above Piedmont in the foothills of the Alps, and these rocky steep slopes produce a slightly different style of Nebbiolo. They also have a Superiore designation, so keep an eye peeled for those.

My favorite wines from Valtellina come from a sub-district called Inferno. These come from a rocky plateau that gets extremely hot, hence Inferno. I hear it is one of the gnarliest vineyards in the world to farm.

Pro Tip: For those of you who like Amarone, they also make a Nebbiolo-based wine in Valtellina called Sforzato, using the same raisinating production method as Amarone.

Another dope choice is Nebbiolo from the Gattinara region (or DOCG). Slightly Northeast of Barolo, here they call the grape Spanna, and label the wines Gattinara. The wines there are a bit lighter, more similar to Barbaresco than Barolo, and delicious.

Pro Tip: there can be some quality variances in Gattinara, but the wines are cheap enough that it's worth taking that risk. In the low $20s they get great, and for $30 you will be able to get a great wine from a great producer, and it will typically have seven to nine years of age on it as well. That same bottle of Barbaresco is $100.

+1 Pro Tip: One of the best producers of Barolo (Roberto Coterno) recently dropped twenty million Euros on a Gattinara winery and vineyards, so I'd expect to see this region taking off in terms of quality and price. Stock up now.

+2 Pro Tip: Some of the Gattinara bottles are made in a special shape that looks like they got left in the sun and melted. That's for trapping the sediment when you pour an older Gattinara. Be sure to bust that little nugget out when you really want to shove your wine-assholery down someone's throat. (For me, this is pretty much all the time, with everyone.)

For our third and final dope choice, we are going to look to Ghemme, which is geographically right next to Gattinara. One major difference though is the soils. Ghemme has much more complex and varied soils than Gattinara. Don't ask me why, that is just how shit works out in Europe.

This soil diversity shows in the wine, where it can create a broader range of flavors and minerality. Wines from here will be labelled "Ghemme".

Pro Tip: I have left out a crap ton of other small regions which all can produce great Nebbiolo. These include Nebbiolo d'Alba, Lessona, Boca, Roero, Bramaterra, Carema and others. I've tried to keep it simple for you all in terms of choices, but you can go way way down a rabbit hole on this (trust me on this one...). But if you are having fun with this, go find some little obscure wine shop and ask for other Nebbiolo-based wine and try whatever they give you. I guarantee it will be eminently drinkable, and likely under $25.

Our specific recommendation this week is straight to Valtellina!

Nino Negri Inferno

Drink Well!

Drinking & Knowing Things
#2: CHENIN BLANC

Ok, I get that Chenin Blanc (which I will abbreviate to Chenin for this discussion) has a bit of a bad rap, particularly in the US. This is primarily because back in the day there were truckloads of a rather ordinary uninteresting value-based jug wine produced labeled Chenin Blanc in the US. So we associate that grape with a rather boring white wine. (Blanc means "white" for you newbies.)

Side Note: A lot of that wine wasn't actually from the Chenin Blanc grape. #marketing

But nothing could be further from the case.

Now, they grow Chenin in many areas around the world, but IMHO there are only two places that make a Chenin worth drinking. The first, and by far the best overall, is the Loire Valley in France. The second is South Africa. Don't bother drinking Chenin from anywhere else.

Why Chenin is Dope AF:

Let's start by talking about styles of Chenin. You can think of them in three categories: dry, slightly sweet, and syrupy. Each are fantastic in their own way. Just don't mix them up. Nothing worse than expecting a dry wine and getting a dessert wine. Or vice versa.

I don't really like talking about "flavors" in wine, because everyone has their own perspective on how they experience smells and what they mean. But I get that it can be helpful – so I'll talk a bit about this WRT to Chenin. For me, I often get a musty flavor similar to chamomile tea on Chenin. Then, I also get some citrus notes, and in riper years some more tropical fruit. For the sweeter styles I often get more honeyed overtones.

Chenin also ages well. Anything older than about five years begins to develop some very interesting complexity. If you are lucky enough to encounter a bottle with twenty years or more of age, purchase it immediately. The firm acid structure lets these wines age remarkably well. And it won't set you back much. As of writing this I saw that Wine Searcher has some 1984 Domaine Huet for $50 and 1995 for $45.

Pro Tip: Be the most interesting person at your next dinner party and roll up with a couple bottles of a thirty-five-year-old Chenin.

Structurally, one of the defining characteristics of Chenin is the acid. Generally, the acid profile is very firm. Moreover, the acid builds in your mouth, like a crescendo. Take a sip of Chenin, and watch how after you swallow the acid continues to increase the watering on the sides of your mouth.

The combination of the acid structure and the fruit profile is what makes Chenin one of the most versatile white wines for food on the planet. You can drink an off-dry Chenin with spicy Thai food (in fact I highly recommend this) or a salad, or a cheeseburger. You can drink a sweet Chenin with cheese or cheesecake.

Pro Tip: any time you are ordering food that feels like it would go well with a white wine, you cannot go wrong with picking a Chenin.

Dope Chenin Choices:

Note that in the Loire Valley (and pretty much everywhere in Europe), all wines will be labeled by the town in which it is produced in (e.g. Vouvray, Montlouis, Coteaux du Layon, Saviennieres, etc.) So it won't say Chenin on the label. You'll either have to know – or ask the somm for a Chenin from the Loire. If you do the latter, make sure you specify dry vs. sweet, depending on what you want.

For dry Chenin my go-to is Saviennieres. These can get a bit pricey. Expect to pay at least $40-60 for a solid Saviennieres. Nicolas Joly is the granddad of kickass Saviennieres; his stuff will be $70 and upwards. But worth it. (BTW I am aware that Saviennieres has one of those little French accent thingies over the "r". But I am not going to try to hunt through the "insert character" function in MS Word to find it and then worry about if it tilts to the left or the right. So don't edit my shit – this is all about content. Not linguistic precision.)

For slightly sweet (or "off dry") Chenin my go-to is Vouvray. The only issue I have with Vouvray is that they make whatever wine they can out of that year's vintage. Many years the wines end up off dry, but not always. Unless you want to become the douchebag who is memorizing vintages from the Loire (and who doesn't?) the easiest way is to ask the person you are buying it from (somm, wine store clerk, whatever). They should know if it is off dry or not. If not, roll the dice. You can easily find great Vouvray under $25, and likely under $20. At least until the Trump wine tariffs completely shit the bed on French wine.

For sweet Chenin there is the broader Coteaux du Layon area, and then a number of smaller areas within that that can also be labelled as such, e.g. Bonnezeaux or Quarts du Chaume. Either of the latter are generally spectacular. The quality of a great Sauternes, at a third or a quarter of the price. Drink these with dessert, or even better as dessert. For $60-70 you can get a Bonnezeaux that will literally blow people's minds.

In South Africa, the Chenin will be labelled as "Chenin" or perhaps "Steen". It is almost always dry (with a couple rare exceptions). Much of it is moderately priced entry level wines, but you can easily find drinkable bottles of South African Chenin for $8-10.

That said, South Africa does make some stellar Chenin. Ken Forrester is a great example of one of these. (Try his FMC Chenin if you can find it.) Generally if you spend $20-25 on a bottle of South African Chenin, you will be getting the high end examples, which will readily compete with $100 bottles of Burgundy or California Chardonnay.

From Vouvray:
Domaine Huet Le Haut-Lieu

From South Africa:
A.A. Badenhorst Secatuers

Drink Well!!

Drinking & Knowing Things
#3: AGLIANICO

Let's talk a bit about Sangiovese. You all know it as the most plentiful red grape in Tuscany, where it is produced in a dizzying array of styles and quality levels across a number of legal areas (or DOC/DOCGs as they are called in Italy). The most prevalent of these is Chianti, and then moving upward in quality and downward in volume, we have Chianti Classico, and then Vino Nobile de Montepulciano, and finally Brunello di Montalcino. All of these wines are made from the Sangiovese grape. There are different price points associated with each area (appellation), but within each appellation there is a fairly wide quality range.

What does this mean? Well, take Brunello as an example. Overall, Brunello produces about 7M bottles a year, and the US imports maybe 25% of those. Some of that imported wine is from the really high-quality producers, and perhaps a tiny percentage are hidden unknown gems. But a large percentage of these are young, heavily oaked wines made to appeal to US palates and primarily for export. So when you see a Brunello on sale at Vons for $29.99 and you think you are getting a bargain – you're not. You're buying the low end of a high-end product. Think of it as buying a 1-series BMW. Yeah, it's a Beemer, but not one that you are necessarily going to enjoy the driving experience and brag to your friends about. It's a Honda Civic with higher maintenance costs.

So what's a person to do, besides trying to learn a bunch of producers and single vineyard examples?

This is where Aglianico comes in.

In my mind, Aglianico is very similar to Sangiovese. The fruit tends to be in the same cherry-ish neighborhood, you get similar herbal and savory notes, and the acid is prominent. The one real difference that I get is on the tannins. Aglianico to me has slightly higher and coarser tannins. In fact, when I am doing blind tasting and I find a wine that I think could be Sangiovese, but the tannins are a bit heavy, I will tend to call Aglianico.

Side note: I did this once in a Master of Wine training session, and not only was I the only one who called it correctly, the instructor called me out and asked me how in the hell I called Aglianico instead of Sangiovese. I'd call that a humble brag, but you all know I haven't passed the final tasting exam yet, so really it is merely me getting one right for a change.

Why Aglianico is Dope AF:

First, it's called the Barolo of the South for a reason. They make kickass wines there. Structurally it probably should be more the "Brunello of the South" but I didn't create the saying. Regardless, the point is that the quality is respected.

Second, it's an extraordinary value. For $40, you are getting the entry side of the Brunello market, but for $40 you can get a very high quality Aglianico. And there are plenty of totally solid Aglianico options available in the $12-18 range. Mastroberardino is typically thought of as one of the very best producers of Aglianico and you can get a current release of their flagship Radici wine for about $50. The high end of the Brunello market is going to be in the $200-$400 range for a current release.

Third, and for me super relevant. Higher end Sangiovese wines, and Brunello in particular, tend to be quite heavy handed with the use of oak. This creates a super oaky wine, which I suppose helps compete with Napa Cabs, if you like that sort of thing. Also, it will help the wine age gracefully for twenty-five years, if you have that sort of time. But if you want to buy a wine and enjoy it immediately, those super oaky wines are not my cup of tea. Aglianico producers (and I would bet that this is due to the economics around producing wine at a lower price point) tend to use more neutral oak and larger oak vessels. Which makes the wine way more drinkable now. However, because of the tannin structure, the wine can still age over a number of years. I've had Aglianicos from the 1990s which were great.

Pro Tip: It's pronounced Al-YAWN-i-ko. At least here in the US. One of my Italian friends who will remain nameless (but rhymes with Lyin' Bidet Yo) consistently argues the point that from a pure Italian perspective the "g" should have a place in the pronunciation. He may be right, but since I am writing this and not him, we are going to do it my way.

Dope Aglianico Choices:

There's only one place to go for Aglianico and that is southern Italy. If you see some cult winemaker from Paso Robles or Chile experimenting with it give it a strong pass. In southern Italy, there are two places of note and the wines will be labeled as such. The first is Taurasi (in Campagnia, for those who give a shit) and the second is Aglianico Del Vulture (in Basilicata).

Weirdly enough, Taurasi is about one-third of the total production volume of Aglianico del Vulture, but for me in California I see Taurasi 90% or more of the time, and rarely see Aglianico del Vulture. I see the Vulture much more often on the East Coast. Hopefully someone from Southern Glazer's reads this and takes immediate action to rectify that giant issue and starts selling more in SoCal.

Pro Tip: The production of Aglianico del Vulture is higher than Taurasi and there is more entry level wine made there. Some of the higher quality wines are actually labeled as a separate DOCG called Aglianico del Vulture Superiore. Keep an eye out for that, and if you see it, grab it. Also, that's a great winedouchey thing to drop on a somm: "Yeah, you got the Vulture, but is it the Superiore?"

I personally prefer the wines from the del Vulture area. To me, they have a bit more savory aspect to them which I believe is due to them being grown on the volcanic soil of the defunct Vulture volcano, which gives a bit more smokiness to the wine. But I drink a shit ton of Taurasi because it is much more readily available in my region.

This week's recommendation:
Bisceglia Gudarra Aglianico del Vulture
Drink Well!!

Drinking & Knowing Things
#4: JURA

Oh, it's $300. It must be good...

The thing is that in wine quality and price are rarely 100% correlated. Rather, the price of a wine is a function of supply and demand. For most terroir-based wines (i.e. from a certain place) the supply is fairly fixed, so if demand goes up, then price increases.

We see this in Burgundy. People tend to forget that in the 1970s, Burgundy had a bad rap. The winemakers used "traditional methods". Which meant throw some grapes in a barrel and come back in a month and put it in a bottle. Without some basic hygiene practices, this created a lot of faulted wine. Back in the day, you could buy Domaine Romanee-Conti for $20 a bottle. Even in the 1980s you could still get assorted cases of it for $750. The lucky fuckers who did that and kept it can now sell that shit for $10,000+ a bottle.

Supply and demand, my friends.

Pro Tip: Those in the know call that wine "DRC".

Which doesn't mean that DRC isn't great. It is. But absent the demand pressures, that wine would be much more affordable. We also saw this with the Chinese interest in first growth Bordeaux, particularly Château Latour and Château Lafite. There's even a Netflix documentary about it called Red Obsession. Check it out.

What annoys me more is Beaujolais. I may have to make this the topic of a future rant. A few years back, I could get a kickass Beaujolais Cru (like a Morgon or Moulin-a-Vent) for $18-20. Then that fucking Somm 2 movie came out and every single somm was like "Beaujolais, Beaujolais, Beaujolais". Now those bottles are $30 minimum. I should have filled up the cellar with that, and made 50% returns on my investment. It wouldn't surprise me if in a few years we saw those going for $60-80.

I'd probably still pay it. I love that shit.

Pro Tip: You may want to consider laying some of that down today and sitting on it for a couple of years. (Past performance is no guarantee of future returns; call a physician if your erection lasts more than four hours.)

But what is next? Where's the next Beaujolais?

I think it could be the Jura.

Why Jura is Dope AF:

OK, let's separate the Jura into red and white. Today we're gonna talk about the reds, but rest assured there will be a future discussion about the whites, particularly Vin Jaune, because that wine is amazing. Stay tuned on that...

The Jura is a small region in France, about fifty miles east and slightly south of Burgundy. (That's ninety kilometers for you Canadians. You're welcome, Magdalena.) For the reds they generally make their wines with two grapes. Poulsard and Trousseau. Yep, I know. WTF are those? Both of these remind me a lot of Pinot Noir. (And they are starting to grow Pinot Noir there as well.) They are both light-bodied wines, with a lot of fragrance, spice, and sometimes some power. The acid is elevated, like a Burgundy, making them both easy drinking wines and also great food pairing wines.

You'll see a range of red wines here, from some that are 100% from one variety and a bunch that are blends. In fact, one great red from the Jura is called the Trio, which is one-third Poulsard, one-third Trousseau, and one-third Pinot Noir. Any of these will have the same characteristics of a solid Premier Cru Burgundy, with a bit more rusticity to them. Which I dig.

Jura is a tiny wine region. In total, they probably make about 300,000 cases of red wine annually, of which maybe 40,000 cases make it to the US. By way of context, that's a little more than half as much red as Caymus produces.

There's a wine geek thing which is to pick the ultimate Thanksgiving dinner wine. Harder than you think, because you have turkey, cranberry, stuffing, mashed potatoes etc. Lots of stuff going on. So it is hard to pick one wine that will complement all the dishes. I have heard Poulsard/Trousseau thrown into this conversation by some uber geeky wine folks. And I agree that this wine has a place in that debate. (For those who give a damn, my horse in this race is sparkling Shiraz. Stay tuned on that one also...)

Dope Jura Choices:

Fortunately, the hipster/natural winemaking/Whole Foods crowd hasn't tumbled onto Poulsard and Trousseau yet, so the only place you can get these is in the Jura. Although I suspect it is only a matter of time before some asshole in Santa Barbara or Arizona is making a shittier version of these but charging three times as much. Fuck that guy. We're still getting ours from the source.

Like everywhere in France, these wines are labelled by the town or area they are from. What we want are wines labelled either Arbois or Cotes du Jura. Both of these regions also produce white wines, so take a close look at the bottle to make sure you are getting a red. (Although the whites are also dope, for different reasons.) The overall availability in the US is meager, but if you find these they generally will be around $20 or even less. And often they will have some bottle age for sure.

> **Side Note:** I have started to see certain Jura producers selling for $40-60 a bottle, which is a trifle disconcerting, a la Beaujolais. I think perhaps some of the US allocations of these wines are really tiny.

> **+1 Side Note:** I recently had a Cotes du Jura from 1969 that was fanfuckingtastic. They can age well. For the record I think I paid about $90 for that bottle. Try that with a fifty-one year old Burgundy.

> **+2 Side Note:** Our good buddy Louis Pasteur (you know him from your milk) grew up in the Jura and owned a vineyard in Arbois that is still rocking today.

Pro Tip: Under no circumstances whatsoever should you buy anything with the words "Macvin" or "Macvin du Jura" on the label. That is fucking garbage wine that is fortified with shitty brandy produced from the leftover trash after fermentation that normal people throw away. Think of it as French Thunderbird. What impresses me is that somehow the producers of this have convinced people that it is special (oh, and it is very special) and consequently they charge three times as much for it. Just don't do it. Unless you are into explosive diarrhea, vomiting, and the shakes. And if that's your thing, listening to Florida Georgia Line produces equal results with less cost and effort.

From a producer perspective there aren't a bunch of options here in the States. There's a few larger houses and they are going to make most of what you will see available in the US. There's also a handful of smaller producers which are starting to become the aforementioned $40-60 crowd. So don't worry about producers. It's gonna be hard enough tracking any of this down.

But as usual, I have made it easy for you. Give this bad boy a try. Or try to get your hands on some of the Trio, made by Berthet-Bondet.

Domaine Roulet Pere & Fils Arbois Rouge

As always, Drink Well!!

DRINKING & KNOWING THINGS

#5: CHAMPAGNE.
YOU'RE DOING IT WRONG...

Champagne is amazing. And multi-functional. As anyone who has read The Champagne Tales can attest to. But most of you plebeians are doing it wrong. Fortunately, you all have my ardor and wisdom to guide you on the path to complete hedonistic bliss.

Before we jump in though, recognize that when I say Champagne I mean sparkling wine made in the Champagne region of France, using the traditional method of aging wine in the bottle, on the lees (which are dead yeast cells).

I don't mean Prosecco, or Moscato, or California Sparkling, or anything else with bubbles. There's nothing worse than asking for a glass of Champagne and being handed a glass of Prosecco. WTF, people? These are very different wines. Not that Prosecco is bad per se, but not what I was expecting. This would be akin to me ordering a coke and being brought an Orange Fanta. And having the person say "Well, we don't have coke but this has bubbles, so I thought..." No. Don't think. Prosecco, like Orange Fanta, has a time and place. But when I want Champagne, I want Champagne. Today we are gonna talk about Champagne.

Why Champagne is Dope AF:
I suppose that there are three defining aspects of good Champagne. First, it has high acidity. Which allows for lots of drinking and food pairing options (as well as completely fucking your GI tract if you drink four bottles of it – or so I have heard).

Second, the aging on lees brings heavy yeast, brioche, and freshly baked bread flavors. The longer the aging, the more the flavor.

Third, it has bubbles! That's always fun.

There's a bunch more complexity than those three things, but that's the basics.

The downside of Champagne is that it is expensive, especially for the really good ones. Also, there's a bunch of confusing different options: vintage vs. non-vintage, grand cru, Brut vs. extra Brut, Grand Marques vs. non-grand Marques, WTF is a blanc de blanc or a blanc de noir, Grower Champagnes, etc. Which makes it tough to know what's worth drinking, or a good value for price tradeoff.

Pro Tip: Many of the "best" Champagnes are not. Veuve Cliquot Yellow Label is one of the shittiest Champagnes of all time for the price. If you drink this, you are a victim of marketing and also an idiot. Here's some homework. Get a bottle of Yellow Label, and also a bottle of something else at the same price point (Pol Roger, Henriot, whatever). Pour a glass of each and drink them side by side. You will immediately notice that the Yellow Label is bitter, tastes rather disjointed and not as smooth, and the bubbles are larger and harsher. Side by side, it's easy to taste the difference. Then enjoy the other bottle while you use the leftover Yellow Label to degrease your lawnmower. Ace of Spades is even a worse deal. This wine used to be $30 a bottle, until they re-designed the bottle and label, and Jay-Z liked it and eventually bought the company. Now it's $750 a bottle, for literally the exact same wine. Genius on their part I must admit. But crappy wine for the price.

Why You're Doing It Wrong:

USAGE:

For some reason, Champagne has become this wine that is synonymous with special occasions, parties, toasts, and as an aperitif to start the evening. It is a great wine for all those purposes. However, Champagne is first and foremost a wine, and has waaaayyyyyy more utility than just those circumstances.

For instance, because of the elevated acidity, and the body that comes from lengthy aging on lees, Champagne makes an extraordinarily great food pairing wine. And there's a wide range of Champagne choices from lighter to heavier body wines, which allows for pairing with lighter foods like salad or oysters, all the way up to foods with heavier sauces. Try Champagne with Fettucine Alfredo, or even a vintage Champagne with steak (trust me, just try it). Also, I think Champagne is a great wine for pairing with desserts. Get a Champagne that says Sec on the label, and try it with chocolate cake or lemon tart. I think Champagne is a much better pairing with chocolate than the traditional Port pairing.

Try having a dinner and only drinking Champagne throughout the whole dinner. You'll be surprised and amazed at how great it is with food. Then rinse and repeat with every meal henceforth.

Pro Tip: This is awesome. Get a nice bottle of Champagne – something simple from a good house. Laurent-Perrier for example. Chill it up. Then go get a bucket of extra crispy KFC and drink the Champagne while smashing through the bucket. It will blow your goddamn mind.

GLASSES:

This is a sore spot for me. I truly don't get this. Recognize that most of how you experience wine is through your nose. We have big tapered wine glasses to concentrate the aromas and funnel them into your nose while you drink them. Except for Champagne.

Champagne generally comes in a flute or a coupe. Both are shit for experiencing Champagne.

The flute provides a long tall narrow glass so you can watch the bubbles go up. Ooooohhh, pretty. Except now the surface area of the wine is the size of a fifty-cent piece. It isn't going to let off much in the way of aromas. Plus, the flute is filled almost to the top, which doesn't really allow you to funnel in what limited aromas are coming off the top, nor can you easily get your nose into the glass.

The coupe, in contrast, is small and shallow. The glasses that they make the Champagne fountains at parties and weddings out of. Ooooooohh, pretty. Except now the surface area represents half the volume of the glass. And it's also filled to the top. All the aromas and bubbles vent out in the first sixty seconds and then you are quaffing flat insipid Champagne, especially if you got a glass from the bottom of the stack, which has been sitting for ten minutes.

Side Note: They say that the shape of the coupe was based on Marie Antoinette's breast. I don't know if that is true or not, but I can't help but have a bunch of questions about that every time I am holding a coupe. You can think about that at every wedding and New Year's from now on. You're welcome.

So what to do? Easy. Just refuse to drink Champagne in either of these glasses. Be a dick about it if you have to – this is Champagne we're talking about after all. A normal white wine glass is perfect; whatever you would drink a decent Chardonnay out of. The surface area will release the right level of aromas, and the sides will funnel those aromas to your nose. Done deal. Make sure if you are in a restaurant that you tell the waiter or somm when you order the wine e.g. "Yo, bring that in a Chardonnay glass" as opposed to after they bring it. You will get instant respect.

Our Weekly Recommendation:

Hard to give a simple recommendation here, but I generally look for smaller, lesser known houses, with good grapes (preferably Grand Cru vineyards) and lengthy aging on lees. These generally aren't always as broadly available. I usually score mine from smaller mailing list allocations. But here's a decent example of a lesser known house with a solid product at a fair price that is widely available.

Gossett Brut Excellence

And wait until next week, when I talk about substitutes for Champagne that allow you the same experience at one-third or one-half the price.

Drink Well.

DRINKING & KNOWING THINGS
#6: CHAMPAGNE, YOU'RE DOING IT WRONG, CONTINUED...

Picking up from where we left off on Champagne last week. Now you are all educated, and have quickly hurled all your flutes and coupes in the nearest receptacle, even the nice hand cut crystal flutes that you got for your wedding toast and which mostly sit unused on the top shelf of your curio cabinet, and only get broken out on anniversaries and special occasions which is – guess what – the only time you drink Champagne.

Now that you are indoctrinated, you don't have to wait for those days. Now you're quaffing Champagne in red Solo cups with your KFC on a Tuesday like the rest of us wine professionals.

Congratulations. You're halfway there.

Our goal now is to find the best possible Champagne experience at the lowest possible price. I'll simplify this as much as I possibly can, and acknowledge that some of you reading this are wine professionals who are going to argue the merits of blending, grape selections, recent disgorgement and so on. If this is you, I am more than happy to spend hours geeking out with you on this. But the rest of you knuckleheads do not give the tiniest shit about any of this stuff, and are like my kids when I help them with their homework.

"Daaaaaaaadddd. Don't explain it to me. I don't care about (insert any high school subject here). Just give me the answer."

My plan is to just give you the answer.

What we want to look for is the longest amount of time possible that the wine has spent aging on lees. We want this to be five years or more.

Note that they generally don't put this information on the bottle. Nor is it necessarily related to how old the wine is. You could have a bottle that spent eighteen months on the lees, and then spent the next twenty years in someone's cellar. Moreover, unless it is vintage, they won't even put a year on the label, so you won't even know that most of the time.

Side Note: For the record, probably the best Champagne I have ever had was a 1983 Dom Perignon, that I drank in 2018. Probably nine years on lees and an additional sixteen years aging in the bottle. Big ups to Abi for a) raiding her dad's cellar and b) being cool enough to share that with me.

Pro Tip: Most people don't know that Dom actually has three levels. The regular Dom which everyone knows is aged on lees for let's say, oh nine years-ish. Then it's labeled and released. But some is left to continue to age on the lees for longer, maybe fifteen years, at which point it is labelled as Dom P2 and released. Some of that is held back to age even longer, and once it passes twenty-five years aging on the lees it is labelled as Dom P3 and released. If you ever see this anywhere, buy it immediately no matter what. Then contact me for my mailing address. No, seriously. I've never even seen a bottle of this in person. I'm dying to get my hands on some. Gonna be expensive but fuck it.

Also another great thing to drop on a somm: "Yo, you got the P2?"

+1 Pro Tip: This whole P2 and P3 thing is pretty new. I don't think they have released any P3 yet, although I have seen (and had) the P2, which is awesome. I think the P3 is still being aged. That said, keep those eyes peeled...

Now, the French have different minimum requirements for aging on lees. For vintage Champagne (often considered the best) the law is a minimum of four years aging, three of those on the lees. This is good. But we want five or more years on lees. Plus, vintage Champagne is super expensive. Krug Cuvee spends six to seven years on lees and is $160+. Bollinger R.D. spends ten years or more on lees, and starts at $200.

Pro Tip: Bollinger R.D. is what James Bond drinks. Just saying...

But for those of us who don't want to be dropping eight hundred smacks every time we smash through four bottles of bubbly with our KFC, are there other options?

Hell yeah there are. Bienvenido a Italy!

Why Italian Traditional Method Sparkling Wines are Dope AF:

They use the same grapes as Champagne, grown in similar climates and made the exact same way. At a fraction of the price.

Some Dope Italian Choices:

Two places here. Franciacorta and Trentodoc. These will be labeled as such.

Franciacorta is great. What we want to look for are wines labelled "Riserva". These wines have a legal minimum aging requirement of sixty months on the lees, two years longer than vintage Champagne. Which is a giant Italian middle finger raised and pointed mockingly directly at the minimum aging requirements of Champagne. Which I think is funny as hell. Bravo, Italy...

Down there, the weather is a tiny bit warmer than Champagne, which means you will get a tiny bit more fruit and a tiny bit less acid. But this is more or less irrelevant for the Riserva, because what we are after is the lees aging, which is gonna drive the profile of the wine much more than fruit or acid.

Franciacorta wines are generally pretty widely available, but the Riserva is much more difficult to lay your hands on. You'll have to do a bit of digging here I'm afraid. Or get a non-Riserva, which will be solid, but not as spectacular as the Riserva. Here's a decent option on a really nice bottle:

Ca' Del Bosco Cuvee Prestige

I'm actually more excited about Trentodoc than Franciacorta. Trentodoc is from the Trento DOC (hence Trentodoc as it is now recently branded, although this branding has caused an absurd amount of confusion). This area is in the North, so it is cooler there and the wine has almost the identical structure as Champagne. Now, let's separate

Trentodoc into two categories. Big producers (there are two – Ferrari and Cavit). And small producers (a ton of little guys). While the big producers produce great wine at good values, they aren't doing anything extra-special on the high end of the market. The little guys on the other hand, are getting after it, and really pushing the quality envelope. Which they kind of have to because no one knows the region. Generally you will find lees aging at the smaller producers of anywhere from seven to twelve years. Much more than all but the most exclusive Champagnes. And at ridiculous price points by comparison. Figure on between $40-50; and for $60-70 you can probably get the best of the best.

Before you start salivating and clapping your hands whilst chortling with glee, note one key fact here.

These wines are a motherfucker to find in the US.

So why am I bothering to tease you all with them? Simple. This is all part of my insidious master plan. If all of you go down to your local wine stores and demand Trentodoc that isn't Ferrari, they will beat on the distributors, and the distributors will go to the importers, and the importers will increase their buys and next year I will have my pick of awesome fucking bubbly at $40. Do your part people...

In the meantime, those of you who have the patience to bang away at Google may able to track some down. Look for producers like Rotari, Endrizzi, and Cesarini. Otherwise, we can always go the Ferrari route, which is pretty available. Recommendation link is below. Absolutely a great wine, but at $65 not quite the super value I am always on the lookout for. I'm curious to see how the prices will start to drop when increased quantities of the little guys' stuff becomes more widely available at half the price.

Ferrari Reserva Lunelli

Drink Well!

Also, I've had a couple requests for creating something where people can share their experiences with these wine recommendations. Since I am way too lazy to build anything elaborate, I set up an Instagram account: @ drinkingandknowing. You can tag your posts here, and also talk shit. First one to post a Franciacorta next to a bucket of KFC wins...

Drinking & Knowing Things
#7: MENCIA

As you all know, I am a huge Burgundy fan. I mean, what kind of obsessive asshole gets a tattoo of the La Tache vineyard across their entire chest? (A: The good kind, that's who...)

But while I adore the wines that Burgundy *can* be, there's some shit going down with Burgundy. Part of this is due to winemakers trying to produce a fuller, richer, oakier style to compete with New World wines, and part is due to global demand driving prices up to levels that become poor values. I have no problem paying $250 or more for a bottle of wine, because I am a baller. If I do, though, it better be kickass. In Burgundy, pretty much anything under $50 is not special – unless you find special gems from unknown producers. And even up to $100-150 can be a bit of a crap shoot.

Now, if you know what you're doing you can navigate the absurd level of complexity that is Burgundy (e.g. the label says Nuits-St.-Georges – is that a village quality wine or a premier cru quality wine?). The savvy French producer knows that you need a PhD in Linguistics allied with a staggeringly comprehensive knowledge of the six hundred forty premier crus there to even try to suss all this out. I think they purposely take lower quality wines and confusingly label them in a way as to make you think they are better than they are.

Recognizing that most of you will never be stupid enough to spend years learning all this detailed nonsense (and getting the occasional full chest tattoo), what can you do? I may be able to distill out some simple recommendations for Burgundy, but that is a future topic (or as like I like to call it – "deferring hard work"). Today we are going to look at an alternative for Burgundy – Mencia!

Side Note: While I also love certain styles of Chardonnay from Burgundy, in this context I am talking about Pinot Noir based wines from Burgundy.

Pro Tip: It's pronounced Menthia. (Mike Tyson voice is optional.) Outside of Spain, most people will not know this wine, and will look at you like you have a speech impediment if you order it using the correct pronunciation. However, this is a secret code that us professional Wineauxs use to determine if you are really one of us, or merely posing and posturing on the periphery (no judgment, Ossher). Up to you if you drop the hard C or not. I, being a general winedouche, always purposefully over-emphasize the pronunciation e.g. Mennnn....Theeee....Ah.

Why Mencia is Dope AF:

There's two styles of Mencia. The first is a super easy drinking almost picnic-style wine. It's light, fruity, with moderate acid and overall a fun wine to drink. Or make Sangria out of, if that's your thing. Or funnel like it's Greek Week. It pairs super well with lighter food.

While I like style one, there is nothing extra special about it other than you can get a great example of this style for under $10, which alone makes it awesome. You'd pay $30 bucks for a similar simple red Burgundy wine (or AOC Borgogne Rouge).

The second style, however, is where shit gets real. There a number of producers who are doing amazing things with Mencia. They're tending old vines, holding yields back, using a bit of oak (but not in an offensive way), doing some careful and attentive wine making, and overall producing some wines that have great balance of delicacy and power, savory spice notes and earthiness, and elegant floral and herbal notes. In other words exactly the same kind of stuff we expect to find in Premier Cru Burgundy, and demand in Grand Cru Burgundy.

Except these wines can be found for under $20. If you drop $30, you're likely getting the best of the best, and for $40, you're getting the juice normally saved for family only.

Done deal, I am all in on Mencia.

Side Note: I always love it when I order some obscure bottle of wine off the wine list, and the sommelier comes running out from the back to find out who the hell ordered the (insert obscure bottle here). This has happened to me on multiple occasions when I have ordered Mencia at a fine dining establishment.

Where to Get Mencia:

There is only one place in the world to get the second style of Mencia, and that is Bierzo, Spain. These wines will be labelled Bierzo (pronounced Biertho, because hard consonants are outlawed in Spain).

(Yes Erik - I know they also make a bit of it in Ribeira Sacra, but I'm trying to make this easy for people.)

Pro Tip: In Bierzo, they often blend a little bit of other grapes in with the Mencia, and sometimes even white grapes. It lets them boost up the color, or florals, or acid, etc to get the exact profile they want. So you definitely get some variation by winemaker. All delicious, though.

There really aren't any dominant producers of Mencia in Bierzo – it's a bunch of smaller family owned wineries. Because I am inherently lazy and always looking for shortcuts as opposed to memorizing tons of producer facts, I generally use a price rule when I am looking at Mencia options at wine shops (doesn't work quite as well in restaurants however). The rule here is:

If it's under $13, it's definitely style one.

If it's over $17, it's definitely style two.

That $13-17 middle range is uncertain, so I kind of stay away from it. I don't want the most expensive simple wine, nor the cheapest complex wine. Unless someone I trust specifically recommends a particular wine in this range I'll tend to stay at slightly higher price points.

The wine below is one of my favorites. This wine was about $22 a year ago and now it is creeping up into the high twenties and low thirties. I'm still gonna buy this up until about $70; it's that good. But I hope it doesn't go that high – so don't buy too much of it. We don't want demand pushing up prices any more!

Raul Perez Ultreia

As always, Drink Well.

And feel free to tag photos of you enjoying these wines @ drinkingandknowing! (That's an "Instagram handle" for you old people...)

DRINKING & KNOWING THINGS
#8: KERNER

Let's all start by agreeing that Riesling is awesome. If you're not drinking Riesling on the regular, then you are excommunicated from the Drinking & Knowing Things crew and are hereby ordered to stop reading these immediately.

We'll definitely double-click on some Riesling topics in the future, but for today, let's stay in obscure grape variety land and talk about Kerner.

Some background on Kerner – it is a man-made crossing of Riesling and an obscure grape called Trollinger (which is an Italian red grape). It was invented in Germany back in the 1920s. It shares a bunch of characteristics with Riesling. Since we have all already agreed that Riesling is awesome, it thereby logically follows that Kerner is probably awesome as well.

> **Pro Tip:** They named the grape "Kerner" after a 19th century poet who wrote bawdy drinking songs. That in itself is enough reason for me to jump on the Kerner bandwagon. But for those of you who need more info, read on.

> **Side Note:** Kit – you may remember we drank two bottles of this on the patio at Big Canyon and this was another one of those moments where someone comes out from the back to see who ordered the (in this case) Kerner. Delicious.

Why Kerner is Dope AF:
Well, as previously mentioned, Riesling is its parent, and it's named after a guy who wrote drinking songs. (For the record, the title of one of his songs translates as "arise, still drunk".) Structurally it has lean acidity, and good stone fruit flavors, making it a great food wine.

Where to Get Kerner:

Kerner was invented in Germany and is pretty widely planted there. I think it is like the seventh or eighth most planted white variety there. However, in my opinion, for some reason the Kerner that grows in Germany never really realizes its full potential. You would more commonly see it in blends rather than as a stand-alone single varietal wine.

One of the reasons that winemakers like Kerner is that it is relatively sturdy and adaptable, so it can be grown in a variety of regions. They grow Kerner all over the damn world even in places like Canada and Japan (hmm, maybe we should consider some Bhutanese plantings...stay tuned). But you've never heard of it, because often people don't list out what is in their blends on the label.

Except in Northern Italy.

Kerner really shines in Northern Italy, where the soil and climatic conditions combine to allow the grapes to reach an exceptional balance of acidity, ripe stone fruit and minerality. Here, they eschew the blends, and instead focus on rich, textured single varietal Kerner. And despite the cool climate, the wines actually reach 13.5 -14% ABV.

And because no one knows about them, they're ridiculously cheap.

Now, Kerner is grown in most of the Northern Italy regions, from Trento to Veneto and Fruili. In my opinion, however, the very best ones come from Alto Adige. Alto Adige has a bit of a love-hate relationship with Kerner. On the one hand, they make fantastic Kerner there, so the locals love that. But it is not as easy to sell, and not as profitable, so they are constantly uprooting vineyards and replanting with stuff like Pinot Grigio. But then people remember how awesome the Kerner can be and then there's a bit of a resurgence. And then the inventory is harder to sell, so back to the replanting we go.

It's a vicious cycle.

But as long as we can still get our hands on some, we're okay with it. This week's recommendation is a Kerner that is made in a monastery by a bunch of monks that have been making wine since the 12th century. So you know it has to be good. And for $20 a bottle, you can load up. Serve it slightly chilled.

Anyway, with that – here's this week's recommendations:

<u>Abbazia di Novacella Kerner</u>

These monks make wines from a whole bunch of other varieties which you may want to check out. They also have a higher end range called Praepositus (which I think is Latin for "kickass wine") that they apply to their better wines from each of the varieties they make. If you want to drop a few more bucks you can give their Kerner Praepositus a shot too.

<u>Abbazia di Novacella Praepositus</u>

Drink Well.

Drinking & Knowing Things
#9: TANNAT

Remember that band you used to love? You put stickers on your car, bought t-shirts, waited in line for hours to buy concert tickets and slept in your car to see them? Then, somehow it faded, and years later you realized that Culture Club, or Motley Crue, or Gene Loves Jezebel or Steve Miller Band or whoever was a pretty shit band. And you wondered why you ever were so wound up about them.

That's part of life. Our tastes and preference evolve over time. In fact, if your tastes and preferences aren't evolving you're not living right.

I see this happen with wine all the time. Especially with me. I see myself today not liking wines that ten years ago I thought were the greatest things ever.

I think that's awesome.

But I recognize that this is not always true for people. I think that people are intimidated by all the different wines, and regions, and stupid descriptor words that they are supposed to know (wait, I don't get pickled gooseberry and flint on this wine like the notes said – am I an idiot?). Instead, they find a widely available wine that they know they like, and then order it all the time. Because it's a safe bet and they won't feel like an idiot when talking to the bartender. While that provides a nice wine experience, it limits your ability to evolve.

You wouldn't eat only one food for the rest of your life, would you? To truly maximize our capacity for loving wine, we need to be continually evolving. In order to be effective with this the Woke Wineaux must do two things:

Have the curiosity to explore.

Be willing to go back later and try again.

I do this constantly. And I am enough of a man to admit when I have been wrong. Let me tell you a little story about Tannat.

Tannat is a highly tannic red grape. Which means it can be bitter and drying in the mouth. Sounds awful, right? Anyway, producers of this wine have experimented with tons of ways to soften the wine and make it more approachable. I, being generally curious about wine, heard about it and immediately sought out some Tannat to check it out.

I hated it.

Ok, I said to myself, maybe I got a bad bottle. Or maybe I don't like this particular producer's style. So I got some more. And hated it again.

Awesome, I said. Mission accomplished. I can now write off Tannat as a shitty grape that I don't like and move on to the next grape. And that's what I did.

Fast forward a few years and I found myself in a small little wine bar in San Francisco which curiously enough specialized in Tannat. Fuck this place, I thought to myself. But I leaned in a bit, and thought, well maybe I will give Tannat another shot. (Truth be told, it was late and nothing else was open.) Talked to the somm and he recommended an older bottle from a good producer (1998 Château Montus, to be precise – I still remember it vividly.)

Drinking it was a gigantic mind fuck. Changed my entire perception of what Tannat could be, under the right circumstances. I recall sitting there holding the glass and thinking to myself about what a judgmental asshole I had been about Tannat.

I love it when life reaches up and visits humility upon you. What a great life lesson!

After that I started drinking Tannat on the regular.

Why Tannat is Dope AF:

Under the right circumstances, Tannat makes this intensely powerful wine with a host of spice and earth character. It kind of reminds me of Barolo, if Barolo was dark as squid ink.

Side Note: one of the reasons why Tannat is so dark and tannic is the thickness of the skins. But the skins are also what contain the antioxidant Resveratrol. Thicker skin = more antioxidants! Consequently, Tannat is a healthy choice. At least that's how I rationalize drinking too much of it. Health first...

Where to Get Tannat:

Tannat basically grows in two places: southern France and Uruguay.

Yeah, that Uruguay. Seems odd but somehow Tannat has become the darling grape of the Uruguay wine scene. Now, I have tried a number of Tannat wines from Uruguay and they don't really do it for me. They are a bit lighter than the French ones; not as powerful. But who knows, maybe in five years I'll try the right one and realize I was being a judgmental asshole again.

So I look to France for my Tannat. Now, it's grown in a few places there, and they also use it to punch up the blends in places like Cahors (ahhhhh Cahors – that's for sure going in a future recommendation – love that stuff). But in my opinion the purest expression of Tannat is from the town of Madiran. And the wines will be labeled "Madiran".

They really have two styles there. A more refined style, which uses more oak, and micro-oxygenation and other modern wine making techniques to make a wine that is more elegant and drinkable when young. These are often blended with a bit of Cabernet Sauvignon or other red grapes to soften it a bit. And a more powerful and intense style that you are gonna want to sit on for a while before drinking.

One of the best producers of Tannat is Alain Brumont. He owns four properties there, with two that trend toward each style: Château Boscasse for the refined style and Château Montus for the more powerful and intense. I love that he is embracing both as opposed to being dogmatic about styles.

Side Note: Alain is widely acknowledged by wine geeks as one of the top winemakers in the world. This dude is kind of crazy deep in the details of grape growing and wine making and does wild shit like pruning his grapes seven times a year.

Here's the Boscasse:

Château Boscasse

And the Montus:

Château Montus

Pro Tip: one recommendation that I heard somewhere along the line and have tried with some great success is to buy a Madiran, open it up and drink a glass. Then put the cork back into the bottle and drink the rest of it four days later. This will help the tannins soften and integrate, particularly helpful with wines that are only two to four years old.

As always, Drink Well.

Drinking & Knowing Things
#10: XINOMAVRO

Picture this situation. You are a small vineyard owner in some older European country. You have been blessed with the family vineyard, that has some magnificent eighty-year-old vines of some local grape, which will typically have a name with a disproportionate number of strange consonants in it (anyone up for a nice glass of Kujundzusa or Txakolina? Yes, those are real wines.)

Now, you can make some interesting wine out of these grapes, but then you can't sell it anywhere. No one outside of your town has heard of it, and we dumb Americans can't even pronounce it. So what do you do?

Well, the first option is to say fuck it, and keep doing what your grandpa did, and make some wine and sell it to your neighbors.

The second option is to rip everything out and replant with Chardonnay or Cab or something that you think can sell. I hate when people do this. But it happens all the time. The world doesn't need another oaky Chardonnay, people. Stop doing this immediately.

The third option is where you invest in some modern technology, and lean in on the local varietal and see what potential can be there to do something amazing. This is dope.

However, the challenge for the consumer is now there are a myriad of choices available, and all of them are weird, and you don't have the time nor the inclination to actually go and try all these wines, and hate a bunch of them just to find some cool shit.

Fortunately, you all know me. I am stupid enough to do this. So today we are gonna talk about Xinomavro.

Pro Tip: It's pronounced kseeno-mav-roe. Which is fun to say. Go ahead, try it right now. Never mind the weird looks from the people sitting around you.

Why Xinomavro is Dope AF:

Ok, first off it is from Greece. Where the locals would argue, with some merit, that they invented wine. (The Romans and the Georgians would disagree with this.) But nevertheless, we have a rich and storied history of making wine there. Now, Xinomavro has been described as the "bastard son of Pinot Noir and Nebbiolo" and I think that is not a terrible descriptor. It is tannic, with high acidity, and some great earthy, spicy licorice notes and red berry.

Side Note: A lot of Xinomavro is grown on the slopes of Mt. Olympus, so you are drinking the same wine as Dionysus did back in the day.

When done well, Xinomavro can be rich, powerful, and an overall delight. But super cheap. Some of these wines can be found for under ten bucks retail. In the US. Which is absurd. I have no idea how they are making any money off of these.

Where to Get Xinomavro:

The birthplace and home of Xinomavro is the Naousa region of Greece. Gotta love the Greeks, they do things their own way. Sometimes the wines will be labeled Naousa, or sometimes Naoussa, or sometimes Xinomavro, or sometimes just a made up name. I'm sure there are actual rules about what has to be on the label but no one seems to give a shit.

Now recognize that in many of these cases these wines may fall into option one above – what I will call "Grandpa's Wine". These are gonna be a bit more rustic in style, which could be good or bad. So going down the Xinomavro rabbit hole can be a bit of a crap shoot. I would love to tell you that I have it all figured out, but I don't. That said, it is fun to try stuff and see what happens. And at these price points there isn't a ton of risk. If you don't like it, pour it on your salad!

Pro Tip: Many winemakers in Naousa are trying to increase the complexity of Xinomavro by blending in a whole slew of other local varieties so you will often find some interesting flavor variations depending on which additional grapes, if any, are being blended in.

And now for the moment you have all been anxiously awaiting: this week's recommendation.

Alpha Estate Hedgehog Xinomavro

Drink Well!

DRINKING & KNOWING THINGS
#11: RIESLING

Holy shit, how good is Riesling? I know of no other grape in the world that is as versatile across a wide range of styles as Riesling, and all of the styles are delicious.

The Good Book is a little fuzzy on the specific details, but I have it on good authority that when Jesus turned water into wine, he turned it into Riesling.

"But isn't that a sweet wine?" (insert your name here) asked. "I don't like sweet wine."

My gut instinct on hearing that objection is: Good. More for me.

But as the World's Leading Wine Influencer I have a responsibility – nay, a duty – to convince you all that you need to step up your Riesling consumption. Because you are missing out.

Styles of Riesling:
Riesling is made all over the globe, and in a myriad of styles. Rather than trying to provide specific details around all the possibilities, let's use a simple three-tier categorization.

Dry

Slightly Sweet

Fucking Syrupy Awesomeness

Why Riesling is Dope AF:
Now, there are some pretty common characteristics across all three categories. Riesling typically gives stone fruit aromas, like pear and apricot. It also often has a distinct petrol aroma (which I agree sounds terrible, but

somehow it is not). The acidity is almost always high, making it a great food wine. One of my favorite all time food pairings is Riesling with spicy Thai food. The acidity also gives it the potential for lengthy aging and development. I've had Rieslings from the 1970s which were spectacular.

Anyway, suffice it to say that whatever you are into wine-wise (dry, sweet, low alcohol, high alcohol, light body, full bodied, etc), there is gonna be a Riesling for you. You just gotta find it.

Now, as previously mentioned, Riesling comes from all over the globe. Matter of fact, there is nothing more terrifying than a Master of Wine tasting exam where eight of the twelve wines are Riesling, each from a different country. And you gotta call the country. You get one wrong, and then that country is off the table, and the cascading effect makes you miss all eight wines. As you get more into Riesling, I strongly encourage you to try Rieslings from different countries. But in the short term, in order to make it easy on you, let's focus our attention on two countries. Germany and Australia.

There's way too much to cover all three categories in one go, so I am gonna break it up. We are gonna start with Dry, and cover the other two next week.

Germany:

Now, in Germany they have a standard industry practice of ridiculously complicated wine laws and classifications, combined with indecipherable labeling requirements. Plus you can have radical climate variation so each vintage can be different. Consequently, it can be super difficult to know if you are getting a Riesling that is dry. Some of the producers have started to put little bar graphs on the labels to show how dry or sweet that particular bottle is. But here's some general guidelines.

First, you can look for wines labeled Grosses Gewach or GG on the label. This tells you the wine came from the very best vineyard sites and that the wine is dry. These are generally awesome. However, they only do this for certain wines. They also have a couple of other labeling systems. Dry wines made under different requirements will be labeled either "Trocken" (for the medium quality wines) or "Kabinett" (for the higher quality wines). Just to make it more confusing, they also sometimes stack "Trocken" onto the higher quality labels, so you could see "Trocken Kabinett" for example.

Pro Tip: Kabinett actually refers by law to the level of sugar in the grapes before fermenting them. Whether or not the winemaker ferments the wine to complete dryness is their specific stylistic choice. So sometimes you will get a Kabinett that is dry, and other times it may be slightly sweet. This is where the bar graph (if they included one), or reading the tasting notes comes in handy if you have a preference for one style over another.

+1 Pro Tip: This is why German wine labeling drives me batshit crazy.

Here's a couple of options for you:

Carl von Schubert Maximin Grunhauser Riesling Grosses Gewach

S.A. Prum Blue Riesling Kabinett

Side Note: The Prum Blue has about 10g/l of residual sugar, so it technically isn't bone dry, although it is below the 12g/l threshold which is usually used to determine if something is "dry". It's gonna have a touch of sweetness. Also, the Prum family has been making Riesling since the 12th century so there is a lot of history in this bottle.

+1 Side Note: Both of these wines are a little pricey for dry Riesling. You can usually find a ton of decent options under $20. These two are both great though and worth a few more bucks.

On to Australia, where things are way easier to figure out. From here you are gonna want to get wines from either the Clare Valley or the Eden Valley. They will be logically labeled as either Clare Valley Riesling or Eden Valley Riesling. (Take note, Germany. Simplicity is dope.)

Both of these valleys will produce bone dry Rieslings with lean acidity and also some hints of lime thrown in with the usual Riesling flavors. Clare is a bit cooler, so the acid will be a bit higher for those, while Eden, being warmer will be slightly more floral. Grab one of each and taste them side by side for an interesting experience on how climate impacts wine.

Now, Jeffrey Gossett is the undisputed Australian Riesling champ, so I can't issue a recommendation that doesn't include him, but his stuff is like two or three times as expensive as everyone else's.

Here's one of his Clare Valley wines:

Grosset Polish Hill Riesling

And here's a great $17 value option from Eden Valley, from another one of the classic producers.

Pewsey Vale Riesling

Drink well my friends. And remember, don't touch your face! (I haven't heard any guidance around touching other people's faces, so I think that is still ok.)

Drinking & Knowing Things
#12: RIESLING, CONTINUED...

Having covered dry Riesling last week we are now gonna discuss the Slightly Sweet and Fucking Syrupy Awesomeness styles. For those of you who proclaim you don't like sweet wines – you are hereby ordered to try these forthwith. They will change your entire worldview vis-à-vis sweet wines.

Why Slightly Sweet and Fucking Syrupy Awesomeness Rieslings are Dope AF:

Both styles have all the great aromatics and flavors of classic Riesling. But they also have a whole additional layer of honey and saffron notes. In addition, the high acidity helps balance the sweetness, so they will be refreshingly sweet without be cloyingly sweet. Because they are Riesling, they are going to pair great with food, or can be enjoyed on their own, particularly as dessert. And generally the alcohol levels are super low, like 8% or even lower, so you can drink them all day long or until the sugar puts you into a diabetic coma.

> **Pro Tip:** If there is any doubt about how amazing these wines can be, note that Egon Muller's Scharzhofberger Trockenbeerenauslese is number three on the list of the world's most expensive wines. Average current release bottle price is $14,000. Take that, Burgundy! (However, it doesn't even come close to making the list of longest fucking German wine names, like Gutsverwaltung Niederhausen Schlossböckelheim Schloßböckelheimer Kupfergrube Riesling Trockenbeerenauslese. Yes, that is a real wine.)

They make both of these styles in many places around the globe, but in the interest of keeping things manageable, we are going to stay (mostly) focused on Germany. Since you read last week's recommendation, you know how damn confusing German wine labels can be. Same rules apply here, but we'll try to keep it as simple as we can.

Slightly Sweet:

The wines that are slightly sweet are going to be labeled either Spatslese or Auslese. As with the Kabinett designation, this labeling by law refers to how much sugar is in the grapes prior to fermentation, not afterwards. Which means the winemaker's personal style choices can provide a range of sweetness levels here. Generally speaking, wines labelled Spatslese are going to be less sweet than wines labelled Auslese.

> **Side Note:** Occasionally a winemaker will decide to ferment Spatslese grapes all the way to dryness. So this isn't a hard and fast rule for determining which wines are slightly sweet, but it works 95% of the time. (Sometimes, they might put "Trocken Spatlese" on the label to identify one of these wines as dry, but not necessarily. Ah, Germany...)

In addition, Germany also has a complicated way of identifying vineyards. For the very highest rated vineyards, the producer can elect to put Grosse Lage on the label. If you see something labelled Grosse Lage Auslese, this means the wine will be slightly sweet and from a "Grand Cru" level vineyard. That said, not everyone uses that Grosse Lage approach, so you could also get a great wine that doesn't have that designation on the label.

Here's an option:

Fritz Haag Brauneberger Juffer Spatslese Riesling

For the value minded folks – here's one under $10.

Schmitt Sohne Piesporter Riesling Spatlese

On to the Fucking Syrupy Awesomeness. These wines are ridiculous. I think these need twenty to thirty years of aging before they even start to reach their potential. When younger the sweetness really stands out, but as they age all kinds of flavors and aromas start to emerge. And the sugar softens and becomes more harmonious.

Where to Find FSA Wines:

Remember, we are staying in Germany for the time being. Which means we have the normal labeling issues to continue trying to wade through. Generally, you are going to look for wines labeled either Beerenauslese or Trockenbeerenauslese. The Trockenbeerenauslese wines will be the sweeter of the two options. God, typing Trockenbeerenauslese repeatedly is a nightmare.

> **Pro Tip:** Perception is everything, so if you want to sound like a winedouche you gotta know the lingo. We usually say "BA" or "TBA" instead of those long-ass words above. Maberry – you would say as follows: "Wale, they-at there-uh is a tay bay ay."

> **+1 Pro Tip:** Austria also uses Spatslese, Auslese, BA and TBA on their wine labels. These wines are also delicious. Just take note when you are looking at labels to see which country it is from. Austria options are going to be way cheaper than their German counterparts. Austria, not Australia. Australia is the place with the easy labels.

> **+2 Pro Tip:** Often the BA and TBA wines are sold in 375ml or 500ml bottles, so don't be surprised when the box arrives and it is a small bottle. Which is fine. You only need like a spoonful.

> **+3 Pro Tip:** Put this shit on top of vanilla ice cream.

Here's some options:

I generally completely disregard any points awarded to any wines by anyone, but especially Robert Parker. But if you are into the point game, he did give this BA wine 100 points. It's a 2017, so you're probably going to want to hold onto this for at least ten years before drinking it.

Markus Molitor Zelting Molitor Beerenauslese

But if you don't feel like waiting a decade, here's a 2006 TBA that is drinkable today.

Dr. Heidemanns Bergweiler Doktorberg Trockenbeerenauslese

And the baller option, a 1990 that is going to be right in the sweet spot of its aging curve. Or you could buy a new Honda Civic. Either way...

<u>Egon Muller Scharzhofberger Trockenbeerenauslese</u>

Drink Well and be distant from others. (I've been emotionally distant for years, it's easier than you think…)

Drinking & Knowing Things
#13: CAHORS

Since we have been self-isolating, I have had the opportunity to catch up on all my Netflix binge watching. Despite how good Tiger King and Don't F*ck With Cats are, one of the shows I was most stoked to check out was Uncorked. Which is a fictional movie about a guy who decides he wants to be a Master Sommelier, and what he does to pursue that goal. I was incredibly excited about it because - hey now, wine is going mainstream Hollywood, directly confirming what I already knew. Which is that wine geeks are the coolest people around (after first responders and medical professionals, of course). I've been trying to figure out who will play me in the DAKT movie. Probably either The Rock or Mark Wahlberg.

Unfortunately, Uncorked falls way short of reality. It's fairly obvious that they had no consulting on any of the technical details. For example, they argue in one scene about whether or not a particular red wine has tannins. They conclude it does not. Sorry folks. All red wine has tannins. And they continually call acid on white wine as medium-minus. Also, not true. Not sure I can think of any white wine at all which has medium-minus acid. And in blind tasting they always call the exact wine by producer. Which everyone knows is damn near impossible. Unless you are a character in the novel Blinders.

What I took away from the movie (which I rate like a C+, but you all have nothing else to do right now, so give it a watch) is that people generally don't know shit about wine. Even those who are writing stories about it.

Except for all of you fortunate souls. Who, thanks to my beneficence, can now both Drink *and* Know Things.

Today you are gonna know things about Cahors.

Why Cahors is Dope AF:

Malbec is a wine most people know. At least they have heard of it. And many of those people would say that the best Malbecs come from Argentina. I will admit that Argentina has adopted Malbec as their national grape, and they do a damn good job of it in some cases. But what people fail to realize is that Malbec is originally from France. It's a classic Bordeaux varietal, and back in the day they used to put a ton of Malbec into Bordeaux wines. Then phylloxera destroyed most of the vineyards back in the 1800s, and when they replanted everything they switched out almost all the Malbec for "higher value" grapes like Cabernet and Merlot.

Except in Cahors.

Now, because it is a Bordeaux varietal, it is going to have a lot of the same characteristics of Cabernet or Merlot. If you like these wines you should dig Cahors. It will be full bodied, slightly spicy, with firm tannins. But since no one knows about Cahors, they are super cheap, especially when compared to Bordeaux, or even higher end Argentinian Malbec.

Pro Tip: Cahors was Ernest Hemingway's favorite wine, and he drank copious amounts of it. Be careful when consuming it or you may find yourself accidentally composing lengthy sagas about old men, and boats, and fishing, and bullfighting.

+1 **Pro Tip:** The wine is often as black as espresso. Which is kind of cool.

+2 **Pro Tip:** It's pronounced Ka-Orr. Not Cay-Horse.

Where to get Cahors:

Cahors is a little town that is a bit southeast of Bordeaux. Wines made there will be labeled Cahors. They don't have any grand cru type of system or any other designations so it will be very simply labeled. Which makes it easy. Recently more and more producers have been also writing "Malbec" on the label because of the commercial success of Argentinian Malbec. These wines are generally exported to America where we are dumb and need to be told what is in the bottle. I have a rule that if it says Cahors Malbec on the label, it probably is the shittier wine that is made in a style that appeals to American palates (think bigger, more voluptuous, more oak) and then exported. I generally don't buy those, and stick to wines labeled Cahors.

Cahors is on a hill overlooking a river, and there are some differences in wine quality depending on where the vineyard is situated on the hill. The sweet spot is kind of in the middle, although people are starting to pay more attention to wines made from grapes grown up on the top of the hill. The crappy part is at the bottom near the river. You're never going to know where the vineyards are located though unless you fanatically study and memorize Cahors vineyard locations, which even I am not willing to do. Your best bet is to try things randomly and see if you like them.

Side Note: World Malbec day is coming up on April 17th, so if you hurry up and order some you should be able to participate. Yes, this is an actual thing.

Our Recommendation of the week:
George Vigouroux Cahors

This is a baller wine to bring to a cocktail party because everyone will be a) this is fucking delicious and b) what the fuck is it, it looks like used motor oil, and c) whoa, wait a goddamn minute - they make Malbec in France? At which point you become the wine hero of the day. You're welcome.

Side Note: This becomes a little more difficult when the cocktail party is done over Zoom.

Pro Tip: Oftentimes they will mix in a bit of Tannat (yay, Tannat!) and/or Merlot into a Cahors. This particular bottle has 5% Merlot in the blend.

Drink Well and stay safe out there!

Drinking & Knowing Things
#14: WINE ETIQUETTE

Bored in quarantine, so I thought I would send out a bonus DAKT this weekend. You're welcome.

I get asked a ton of questions about wine etiquette. I'm rather amused by these. Somehow, in the US we made wine etiquette this huge intimidating thing, like meeting your in-laws for the first time, and desperately wanting to not fuck it up. Everywhere else in the world is like, yeah whatever, slap a jug of wine on the table. And they have fun with it – like in Spain where a traditional *porron* is used like a giant wine bong and passed around social gatherings and everyone gets drenched with wine and laughter.

Those of you who have been to a wine party at my place know exactly what I am talking about.

Anyway, as the World's Leading Wine Influencer, I thought I would take this opportunity to talk about some hard and fast rules that are easy to follow, and will make you much more comfortable about how you enjoy your wine.

Rule 1:
There are no fucking rules. Do whatever you want. Drink however you want. I routinely put ice cubes in wine, even reds. I drink Champagne with steak and red wine with fish. I drink wine out of plastic cups. If a wine needs to open up I will hyperdecant it in a blender. I'll put my hand over the top of the glass and shake it like a ShakeWeight to get more oxygen into it. I drink port before dinner, and Chenin after dinner. I mix red wine with Coke to make a Kalimotxo (these are delicious btw).

If there's ever been any Rule quoted by any wine source ever, I guarantee you I have broken it on multiple occasions. With gusto.

The only people that would give a shit about the "wine rules" aren't people you want to hang out with anyway. Moreover, if you have been following your DAKT recommendations and ordering things like Mencia and Aglianico in front of your friends, and drinking bubbles out of a Chardonnay glass, people are going to assume that you are in the know on some secret wine shit (which essentially you are). Therefore anything that you do is going to be considered some next level stuff. Which gives you carte blanche to do whatever.

I'm always amazed when I am doing something stupid with wine, like dumping a bit of white wine into a glass of Syrah to see if I can make a ghetto Cote-Rotie and everyone is like, oohhhh, Mike is doing it so it must be some MW cool thing to do. And then they try it. But half the time I am just fucking around trying stuff to see what happens.

Rule 2:

Flavor and aroma descriptors are more or less bullshit. Every single one of us experiences wine differently. Some of this is nature, some is nurture. For example, if you grew up in France eating oranges and I grew up in Cali eating oranges, we would have very different ideas about what an "orange" flavor was. So someone from France could be all "hey, I get orange" and I wouldn't have the same experience. Secondly, genetics plays a part. For example, there's a compound called rotundone in Syrah that smells like black pepper. Except about 20% of the population can't smell it. So they will never get that tasting note.

How many times have you read a tasting note, or listened to someone talk about wine, and been all "Hey I don't smell any licorice, or violets, or snozzberries on this." And when that happens you feel like a worthless piece of crap and a wine novice and you keep your mouth shut to avoid being judged by your judgey friends. (If this happens, get new friends.)

The good news is now you don't have to worry about that. You can smell and taste your wine and see what your personal experience is. If it reminds you of something, like violets, cool. If not, no big deal. If people are being assholes about it, sometimes I will make stuff up, and be all "No, I get cinnamon, raspberry jam, extruded coal and overripe quince." Then

I watch them root around in their glasses feeling stupid because they don't know what a quince is.

The point is to not take it too seriously. Whatever your experience is – those are the correct descriptors for you.

But it is awesome to try to lean in and be thoughtful about what your experience is for you. Here's some homework. Get a bottle of New Zealand Sauvignon Blanc. Doesn't really matter what it is or what price point. Kim Crawford is fine. Then pour a glass and take a big sniff. You will likely get a very green smell, like bell pepper or grass or asparagus. Then try to associate it with what YOU think it smells like. Whatever you come up with is the right answer for you.

Rule 3: Snort and Slurp

Remember when Randy in A Christmas Story ate like a pig and got dinner all over his face? That's how you want to enjoy wine. Revel in it. Get dirty. Immerse your senses in it. Remember, most of how you experience the flavors of wine are through your nose, so take a moment and dunk your nose in the glass and take big sips of air through your nose. If you don't identify with any of the aromas, no big deal (see Rule #2).

And slurp! When you slurp it forces oxygen through the wine and aerates it. Think of it as a mini-hyperdecanter in your mouth. It will release all the flavors and aromas.

Which brings us to homework #2. Get a bottle of any red wine you have lying around the house. Pour a glass and take your normal sip. See how you experience the flavor. Then take another sip of wine but don't swallow it. Hold it in your mouth and look down at the ground. Purse your lips and suck some air into your mouth like you're sucking a straw. And see what happens.

You may want to have someone videotape you doing this the first time. Feel free to share these for everyone's amusement. Then repeat this process with every sip you take for the rest of your life.

I snort and slurp all the time and I don't even think about it. It's automatic. But occasionally I will wonder if I've ever sat next to someone at a restaurant or something and totally grossed them out. Then I remember that I don't give even the tiniest of shits even if I did and I go on with my day.

If you're still not convinced, go hang out with a group of MWs and listen to them taste. You would swear you were in a swine feedlot somewhere.

Rule 4:
Drink Well! And stop asking me wine etiquette questions! There is no such thing.

Drinking & Knowing Things
#15: CABERNET FRANC

I'm sure that you all, like me, are spending a fair bit of time these days on Zoom-based happy hours. In fact, I know you are because a boatload of you have been showing up on the DAKT Live happy hours on Fridays. Recently, I found myself having a spirited debate over Zoom about Cabernet Franc with my gun-loving wine-crazed homies from Texas. Which from here on out I will call Cab Franc because a) it is easier and b) that's the lingo, learn that shit.

Anyway, we were having a discussion about it. I was doing my best to explain how fucking amazing Cab Franc can be under certain circumstances. However I must point out that by this time we had already consumed what can only be construed as a "metric fuckton" of wine, and my grandiloquence was, shall we say, not up to the DAKT standard of excellence. In order to rectify this situation, as well as the glaring lack of wine understanding in Texas, I am now using the power of the pen to convey the gospel of Cab Franc. The rest of you get to tag along for shits and giggles.

> **Side Note:** Cab Franc is Ann's favorite wine by a fairly significant margin, and she is knowledgeable enough about wine that her opinion counts. She is annoyed that it took me fifteen DAKT recommendations to get around to Cab Franc.

> **+1 Side Note:** It's also Erik's favorite wine. But in this case one must consider the source.

> **+2 Side Note:** Remember that wine that Paul Giamatti hoarded until the end in Sideways? Sixty percent Cab Franc in that blend. Just saying...

Why Cab Franc is Dope AF:

Cab Franc is a lighter bodied red wine with beautiful perfumed aromatics. It generally has an herbal character to it, and can be both powerful and elegant. Tannins are going to be medium at best.

Note that I continue to use the term "can be". Cab Franc can also be cheaply made or overextracted and/or underripe, at which point it can taste like someone mixed Luden's Cherry cough syrup with cheap vodka and jalapenos and tossed a dollop of dishwashing soap in to top it off. This is another one of those wines that is easy to pre-judge as crappy if you haven't had a good one.

Side Note: One of the wines that is in my Top Ten Ever wines (which really there are like forty wines that make this list, but you get the gist) is a 2008 Clos Rougeard Cab Franc, which Ann and I drank at Clos Maggiore in London, during arguably the best lunch I have ever had in my life.

Pro Tip: Cab Franc is a Bordeaux varietal, and is mixed into Bordeaux style blends around the world – from Bordeaux, Napa, South Africa, Chile, Australia, etc. Pretty much everywhere that makes a Bordeaux blend is gonna put some Cab Franc into it to boost the aromatics. But in this case we are talking about wines that are 100% Cab Franc.

+1 Pro Tip: I think that one of the reasons that there are a bunch of shitty Cab Francs out there is that producers of Bordeaux style blends grow Cab Franc grapes, and in some years they don't need to put that much of it into the blend. Maybe the Cab Franc that year wasn't that great, or maybe they only needed a little of it or whatever, so they bottle up the rest as a single varietal wine so it doesn't go to waste and they can recoup a little cash from it. And it isn't awesome. You'll know because the winery one year will have a "special bottling" or "limited release" or something like that, which will sound very impressive and will magically be a single variety Cab Franc. Avoid these like Coldplay.

Dope Cab Franc Choices:

There's only one place where single variety Cab Franc can be consistently kickass and that is in the Loire Valley in France.

As you all know by now if you have been studying your DAKT, wines in France are labeled by the area or town they are from. There are a shitload of little towns in the Loire which produce Cab Franc. In my opinion the best come from two places: Chinon and Saumur Champigny. They will be labeled as such.

Pro Tip: Saumur Champigny is a subzone within Saumur. Some of the wines labeled simply Saumur are kickass too.

+1 Pro Tip: Both of these towns produce a little bit of white wine, which will also be labeled Chinon or Saumur. Give the bottle a look to make sure you are getting the red wine. Not that the whites are bad, just not what we are looking for today.

Now, one of the awesome things about the Loire is how inexpensive the wines are. It's mostly small family wineries making wine generally for domestic consumption. But what happens is that you definitely will get some quality variation here. Some of the producers are cranking out volumes of wine, while others are being a bit more ambitious and trying to make something special.

Which means Chinon is one place where a price rule can be used with some reasonable accuracy. If's it under $20, it's gonna be a 50/50 crap shoot. Over $20, and you are probably getting something solid.

Side Note: When all this Covid BS ends, and if the restaurants of the world actually survive, and if you happen eventually to find yourself in Manhattan – there's a joint called Racine which has a ridiculously huge wine list of awesome Cab Francs from the Loire. Literally pages of them. Check that shit out. Food's decent, wine's great.

Finally, this week's recommendations!

Our first is from Bernard Baudry. These guys focus on selecting the best grapes from individual vineyards and parcels and are super into sustainability. Plus they were totally cool to us when we showed up on their doorstep during the middle of harvest and they still showed us a great time even though they were super busy. All their wines are solid and they are good people. This is one of their less expensive wines, but if you have a hankering to spend a bit more just search for Bernard Baudry.

Bernard Baudry Les Grange Chinon

On to Saumur Champigny. These wines are going to be a bit more expensive and a bit harder to find. But worth it. In my opinion, Saumur Champigny always brings it. There seems to be less quality variation here than in Chinon. I will almost always pick a Saumur Champigny over a Chinon.

This particular bottle is little pricey but fantastic.

Thierry Germain Les Memoires Saumur Champigny

As always, Drink Well!

DRINKING & KNOWING THINGS
#16: VERMENTINO

I firmly believe all wines have some sort of purpose to them. It's on me to figure out what that optimal usage is. This understanding usually comes from trying a bunch of options that don't work before landing on one that is Dope.

I also believe that the optimal purpose of a wine, like flavors and aromas, is completely individualized. Therefore, I'll listen to opinions about the optimal purposes for specific wines, and I'll give them a try, but I won't take it as dogma.

Example: everyone (maybe not everyone but lots of wine people) will talk about pairing Port with chocolate like it is some sort of multi-orgasmic experience. Maybe it is for them, but I fucking hate it. Port is pretty tannic, which means it has bitter elements to it. Chocolate is also bitter, especially the artisan chocolates. So now you're pairing bitter with more bitter. Secondly, port is sweet. Guess what else is sweet – fucking chocolate. Now you are also pairing sweet with more sweet. There's no complexity or complementariness to it. You're just doubling down on bitter and sweet. Blechhh. (I mean, I'll still do it. I just won't like it very much...)

I don't get it. For me, anyway. However, if you find a wine pairing or wine that you like and works for you, cool. You're ahead of the curve. Unless it is Rombauer Chardonnay. Then you should immediately throw that in the garbage and find something that isn't shitty.

My goal is to find how to enjoy certain wines. Sometimes that answer comes very easily. Which brings us to Vermentino.

Why Vermentino is Dope AF:

Sometimes I am in the mood for rich, complex wines that require a lot of my attention. Sometimes I want something simple and delicious and super easy to drink. However, I don't want these wines to be boring. I still want them to have some interesting aromas and flavors, and also be eminently quaffable.

This is where Vermentino comes in. It's a white wine with high acidity and aromatics. It kind of reminds me of Sauvignon Blanc, if Sauvignon Blanc had a lot of minerality and sea spray mixed in with it. And didn't taste like green. Drinking Vermentino is like eating a sweet Meyer lemon on the Newport Beach Pier while smoking a Cohiba.

It's so fucking tasty and easy to drink.

Vermentino has over the years become one of my go-to wines for drinking in the afternoon sun. Whether I'm sitting out back by the pool, or down at the beach, or at a backyard BBQ, or a baseball game, or on a cruise (just kidding, you would have to be a total moron to go on a cruise). Point is IMHO the purpose of Vermentino is day drinking in the sunshine.

Because of the elevated acid it is also gonna pair well with food, but I never really drink it with food unless it is sunshine day drinking food like nachos or fish tacos.

Where to get Dope Vermentino:

One place only. Sardinia. (As the World's Leading Wine Influencer, I will also decree an exception for a couple of guys on Corsica who are making some awesome stuff there.)

If you are American, this means that you don't know geography, and therefore don't know where Sardinia is. It is a large island off the coast of Italy, north of Sicily.

They also make Vermentino on mainland Italy, as well as in other areas here and there around the world. In fact, in Provence the French sneak some of it into the Rosé, but they don't really talk about it that much because it is an Italian grape. Don't ask them about it either. They'll get annoyed and will debate you for hours on the DNA parentage of their Vermentino, which they call Rolle so no one will know it is Vermentino.

But there is something about the combination of the proximity to the ocean and the soil on Sardinia that makes the Vermentino there reach its full potential.

On Sardinia, they make regular Vermentino all over the island. These are cheap (often under ten bucks), simple and delicious. They will be generally labeled Vermentino de Sardegna (I don't know why the Italians insist on spelling Sardinia wrong, but they do.)

Here's a great option.

Cantina Argiolas Costamolino Vermentino

At $14, you can't go wrong with this. Grab a case and your Saturday afternoons are set for the next two weeks.

They also have a special area (a DOCG) called Vermentino di Gallura. These wines tend to have a bit more complexity. And like a number of Italian wines, this DOCG also has a Superiore designation to indicate the best of the best. Remember to drop this on the somm just to be a dick: "Yeah, but is it the di Gallura Superiore?"

Here's a fantastic bottle.

Piero Mancini Vermentino di Gallura

Drink Well!

Drinking & Knowing Things

#17: GIGONDAS

One of my favorite wine regions is the Rhône Valley. Yeah, I know. I seem to have like fifty favorite wine regions, but for different reasons. It's like shoes. You need specific shoes for work, but different colors and styles to complement different suits. Then some casual shoes for tooling around on weekends. And at least one pair of Vans is mandatory. And yeah probably some running shoes, maybe one pair for trails but a different pair for the street. And maybe some gym shoes. And some special purpose shoes that you only break out once in a while but are super important in those circumstances. Like tuxedo shoes or golf shoes or motorcycle boots.

And you gotta use the right shoes for the right occasions. Plaid Chuck Taylor All-Stars with a picture on the side of Sid Vicious flipping the bird (yes, I have these) make you look like an asshole when paired with a suit. Those same shoes on a skate ramp make you the dopest old guy on the ramp.

I treat wine the same way I treat shoes. I'm gonna break out a PX sherry now and then, but only for certain gangster circumstances. Riesling on the other hand is like flip-flops. Suitable for daily use. So the Rhône Valley is one of my all time go-tos for certain things. If you aren't drinking Rhône juice on the regular you are hereby forbidden to drink Riesling as well. And immediately unfriend me on facebook.

Why the Rhône is Dope AF:
Well, there's a lot of shit going on in the Rhône. They produce about 650M bottles of wine annually. That is literally almost half as much wine as the entirety of Australia produces. In a region that is about one hundred twenty miles long. It's pretty jammed with wineries. They make wines of all shapes and sizes there, both red and white, dry and sweet, from

$2 a bottle up to thousands of dollars a bottle. Pretty sure there's a wine for you somewhere in that spectrum that you are gonna dig.

This region is just above Italy. When then Romans conquered most of Europe, they planted a ton of grapes as they went along, because wine is good for fighting. Rhône was pretty early on in this timeline, which means they have a two thousand year history of making wine.

They grow a bunch of grapes there you have heard of, like Syrah or Grenache. And a bunch you have never heard of, like Bourboulenc and Clairette. And they grow them in towns you have heard of, like Châteauneuf du Pape (I mean, even the Beastie Boys name-checked CDP in Body Movin'), and a bunch of towns you never heard of, like Lirac.

The Rhône is way too fucking huge for me to write a single recommendation on it. Consequently, I am going to break out a few of the wines that are seriously kickass. Today's class focuses on Gigondas.

Why Gigondas is Dope AF:

One of the most famous wines from the Rhône is a blend of Grenache, Syrah and Mourvèdre. This is so popular around the world that even Olive Garden waiters and Mr. Humphries know it by its abbreviation – a GSM blend. GSM blends tend to be fairly high in alcohol (bonus!), with a range of red fruit flavors and tannins depending on what grapes they put in the blend. They make GSM blends all over the southern Rhône, in a wide range of quality and price levels.

> **Pro Tip:** You would say Gee-Ess-Emm blend. Do not treat it like an acronym and say "Jism" blend. If you ask a waiter for this you may get something unexpected. I think this could possibly be why Mr. Humphries is familiar with this wine.

Now, GSM blends in the Rhône are allowed to have up to like twenty different grapes in them. But most places focus on the main three: Grenache, Syrah, Mourvèdre. You have heard of the most famous GSM blend – the aforementioned Châteauneuf du Pape. Now, I like me a good CDP. But I don't like the prices. For me, I think the price to quality ratio for CDP is often a bit out of whack.

Enter Gigondas.

Gigondas is a little town about thirteen miles north of CDP. Like CDP it is known for making high enough quality wine that they can label the wine by the name of the town. They specialize in GSM blends. The town just isn't as well known as CDP, because the Pope never had a summer home in Gigondas back in the day.

Pro Tip: In CDP, the blends are all over the place in terms of what grapes go into the mix. In Gigondas, Grenache is almost always the dominant grape.

Pro Tip +1: My MW mnemonic for this is that both begin with a "G". For the Franklin and Marshall grads a "mnemonic" is a fancy word for something that helps you remember.

Gigondas makes beautiful red berry wines with soft perfume, moderate body and soft tannins. I dig them because in my opinion they are not as big and overblown as a lot of CDPs are. Also, they tend to use very little new oak in Gigondas, so the wines aren't overoaked. Which in addition helps keep the cost down. For $30 you can get a spectacular Gigondas, whereas $30 might get you the most basic entry level CDP.

Side Note: It is super hard to spend more than $50 on Gigondas. I have tried many times. However, there are a couple of smaller producers who produce some absurdly good wine in the $100+ range that in my opinion kick the living shit out of higher end CDPs at two or three times the price.

On to our recommendations. The first is a standard, high quality, reasonably priced option

Domaine Les Pallieres Gigondas

The second is for ballers only. But trust me – for $100 this wine is amazing. You all know my feelings about point scores (they're bullshit, in case you forgot). However, I do take notice when the "experts" are dropping ninety-seven and ninety-eight point scores on a wine I like. This same scoring Napa Cab would be $500+.

St. Cosme Le Claux Gigondas

Pro Tip: This latter recommendation is probably still a trifle too young to drink. It might need another year or so before it starts to emerge.

Drink Well!

DRINKING & KNOWING THINGS
#18: SPARKLING SHIRAZ

You see, my faithful DAKT Disciples - highly skilled writers like myself, David Foster Wallace, and Charles Dickens use an advanced technique called "foreshadowing" to suck the reader in, get them emotionally invested, and make them unable to sleep at night because they are all aquiver with anticipation. This is where I mention something in an earlier DAKT and then dick tease you with it for weeks before finally delivering the goods. And it is so, so much better for you, having waited patiently. You're welcome...

In this case, I know you all have been eagerly waiting for me to finally get around to the discussion about the perfect Thanksgiving wine which I foreshadowed in my seminal work DAKT 4: The Jura. Your hopes and prayers are about to be answered.

Think about Thanksgiving dinner. You have turkey, which is a white meat. But is going to be a heavier white meat. You're gonna need a wine with a bit of power to it. But not something with tannins that are too heavy. But wait! There's also gravy, which is going to be fatty, so some acid is gonna be welcome. And also cranberries, which are going to be sweet. And stuffing which is essentially soggy croutons with a couple of random pieces of celery. We need something to complement that. And probably some green beans, so we need a wine that can go with vegetables without overpowering them. Shit, we forgot about the mashed potatoes. That's gonna need something reasonably neutral. And then we also have...

You can go down a gigantic hole on this. The bottom line is that you really need like five or six different wines, where you have a glass of each next to your plate and drink from depending on which dish you are taking a bite of. Unless you are one of those mouth-breathers who mixes all your food together, which is just wrong.

Pro Tip: Six different wines is how I do it. But for all you rookies and dabblers who aren't willing to pop six bottles of wine in order to have the perfect Thanksgiving Day chow fest, read on.

The bottom line is that there is no solution to this problem. It is impossible to find a wine that is going to complement everything at Thanksgiving. Which makes it a wonderful debate topic. You can at any moment or situation toss this question into a group of Wineauxs and spirited conversation will ensue for at least an hour. It's unsolvable, like the Why Does Nickelback Exist? conundrum.

But we all have opinions about it. Fortunately, you all have insider access to the World's Leading Wine Influencer. You no longer need to be fettered with the opinions of assholes and ignoramuses. You can trust that whatever I say is exactly right and the only opinion that is relevant, and you can use your new found knowledge to uncork a bottle of wine whoopass the next time you are surrounded by these cretins.

The answer is simple: Sparkling Shiraz

Why Sparkling Shiraz is Dope AF:
Let's begin by describing what sparkling Shiraz is. Shiraz what the Aussies call Syrah. Same grape, but different name. Crocodile Dundee accent is optional. (That's not a wine, this is a wine...) It is a big, heavy, powerful, high alcohol red wine with firm tannins.

Now, you may be familiar with Australian Shiraz. This is a wine with some pros and cons. It could conceivably make the DAKT roster sometime, but that's a hard maybe. Not sure it clears the Dope AF requirement. I'll have to think on that. But sparkling means exactly what you think it does. They take a regular Shiraz, and then do a secondary fermentation in the bottle, exactly like they do in Champagne.

So what the fuck is it? It's not a sparkling wine, not really. It's way too big and powerful for that. But it isn't really a big wine because it has bubbles in it, and is kind of fruity and perhaps a touch of sweetness. And it has a freshness and crispness about it that you wouldn't really expect from a red wine, particularly an Australian red wine. Which makes it good with food. But it is too sweet and bubbly to stand against a steak, but too big for a dessert wine.

I could go on all day. The reality is that sparkling Shiraz is a category all on its own. It's unique. But for some reason it works amazingly well with Thanksgiving dinner. I think the fruitiness works with the cranberry, the acid works with the gravy, the body works with the turkey and the bubbles work with the celebratory nature of the day.

Pro Tip: I shouldn't even have to say this. But don't put this shit in a Champagne flute or coupe. Use a big red wine glass.

Side Note: I once did an event with a Girl Scout cookie and wine pairing (which was way fucking harder than I had anticipated) and I ended up pairing Thin Mints with sparkling Shiraz. Winner!

Now for some good news. You don't need to wait until Thanksgiving to drink sparkling Shiraz. You can drink it whenever the fuck you want. You're an adult.

That said, it's a bit of an odd wine. It's so big and hearty that if you relax with a glass in the afternoon, one glass is all you need. The second glass is going to get a bit cloying on you. It kind of cries out for a food accompaniment, but needs some variety. So it's a bit tough to figure out exactly the best usage for it outside of Thanksgiving, or maybe Thin Mints.

Pro Tip: One of my favorite ways to enjoy sparkling Shiraz is as an aperitif. Get a bottle for your first post-lockdown dinner party and pour everyone a small glass before dinner. It will be enough to get everyone's gastric systems working, and will also pique their interest as in, hmm what the fuck was that? Looks like it might be an interesting evening after all...

+1 Pro Tip: It also makes a fantastic Sangria.

Where to get Dope Sparkling Shiraz:

Australia. 'Nuff said. No one else in the world has managed to make a drinkable sparkling big red wine. I'm not even sure how these guys pulled it off. This is one of those "whose idea was this anyway?" kind of wines that actually worked. I'm guessing the first batch might have been made by accident where someone forgot to filter the Shiraz which then fermented again in the bottle and then some guy named Big Tom or something drank it anyway and was all "crikey lads, this is some ace plonk".

Side Note: That's how White Zinfandel was created. True story.

Before we get to this week's recommendation, let me provide some guidance here. They do make two different types of sparkling Shiraz. One is bulk volume stuff which tastes like carbonated grape juice and isn't very interesting. You can make this yourself at home if you have a bottle of cheap Shiraz and one of the SodaStream things. (Pro Tip: Don't.)

The other type is more of a quality wine which goes through secondary fermentation in bottle. The easiest way to tell which is which by the price. You are going to want to stay away from anything under $14. Over that and you should be fine.

This week's recommendation is in that second category and is ambitious. Give it a go, mate.

Best's Great Western Sparkling Shiraz

As always, Drink Well. Or Good on Ya...

Drinking & Knowing Things
#19: BANDOL

It's amazing to me how much of the wine world is brand and trend driven. It's almost as ridiculous as the fashion world. Some new fad pops up, e.g. Rosé, and next thing you know everyone is drinking it, the prices go up, and a bunch of new producers hop into the space and start pumping out volume. Now we have a shitload of Rosé available at the local Pavilions. Most of it is blah. The stuff that is good is priced 50% higher than it was last year.

If Rosé wasn't the bomb, I'd probably stop drinking it for a while until the market equilibrates. But summer beckons, and I live in Southern California...

As the World's Leading Wine Influencer, on the one hand I am stoked to see more people excited about enjoying wine and trying new things. But selfishly I also want to drink well at the lowest possible price. The good news is that once this Rosé thing has run its course in another year or so all the newcomers will drop out of the market, and the prices will come back down.

Sometimes that doesn't happen though. The wines come into favor and just keep going up in price. Like Burgundy and Bordeaux.

One of my main goals is trying to find those wines that are fanfuckingtastic that either a) no one has heard of, or b) maybe once they were a fad but then interest waned. Either way, I want to have the maximum possible wine enjoyment at the lowest possible price.

Enter Bandol.

Why Bandol is Dope AF:
Back in the day, there were commonly held to be five "noble wines" of

Europe. For your convenience, they all start with a "B". Four of these you have heard of: Burgundy, Bordeaux, Brunello and Barolo.

Pretty kickass list, right?

The fifth is Bandol.

For many years, Bandol was considered to be among the top red wines of the world. And then somehow along the way it fell out of favor. Which doesn't mean it isn't great. It still is. What it means is that a glorious opportunity exists for us to have an awesome red wine at a much lower price point than the equivalent level of quality from one of the other B's.

Bandol is a small town in Southern France, near Marseille on the French Riviera. It gets a crapload of sunlight combined with moderating sea breezes which allows the grapes to develop a unique set of flavors. They grow a handful of different grapes there, but the Rockstar grape is Mourvèdre. Yep, the M in your GSM blend.

In my opinion, single varietal Mourvèdre reaches its most pure expression and quality in Bandol. You will get black fruit flavors, firm tannins and a whole host of other flavors like licorice, tobacco, spice and earth. When done correctly, Mourvèdre makes one of the finest red wines in the world. In fact, the first wine I ever made was Mourvèdre, which I sourced from Snake River Valley in Idaho and which ended up being not the purist expression of Mourvèdre on the planet...

Where to Get Bandol:
From Bandol. Duh.

That said, we do want to be a bit careful here. Any wine made in the town can be labeled Bandol, as long as it is made from one of the allowable grapes, Not everything labeled Bandol is Mourvèdre dominant. The whites in particular are uninteresting, which is a pleasant wine euphemism for shitty.

Pro Tip: They also make a Bandol Rosé which is phenomenal and probably my favorite Rosé. Stick with these or the big reds.

Now the granddaddy of Bandol is Domaine Tempier. They make a range of wines, including three different big reds from different parcels (my favorite is the La Tourtine, for what it's worth). The best Bandol I have ever had was an aged Domaine Tempier. And the first bottle Bobby and Trilby drank in Double Blind was a Domaine Tempier. It's good shit. I can't have a conversation about Bandol without including them.

However, my Tempier discussion comes with a caveat. I think their quality control processes suck. In my experience about one out of every three or four bottles from Tempier is faulted. Sometimes it's too much brett, sometimes cork taint, and sometimes it just tastes bad. You're taking a gamble with it. It sucks to buy a case of wine and have to waste three bottles pouring them down the sink. (Which is why I never do it, I just serve them to those of my guests like Sulak who won't know any better.) If you try a bottle of Tempier Bandol and you don't like it, it may be that you have gotten a bad one. It's like playing the lottery with $80 and a two-thirds chance of winning. You gotta play it a couple of times before you make up your mind.

Side Note: Robert Parker, who is an asshole and singlehandedly ruined Cabernet with his point ratings, once proclaimed Domaine Tempier's Rosé as the best in the world. I hate it when I agree with anything that tool says, but he was spot on with that one.

Pro Tip: These wines need some age. I try to never drink a Bandol red unless it has a minimum of six or seven years of age. The Rosés however can be drunk immediately.

On to our recommendations:

We're gonna start with what I am now going to call the "lottery" wine. Put your $80 on the felt and see what happens. Note that this particular wine is a 2017, so you may want to hang on to it for a couple of years before finding out if you won the bet. Wine's not a game for the immediately gratified.

Domaine Tempier Bandol La Tourtine

But if you don't feel like playing the lottery, here's one for half the price that is delicious and one of my go-to producers. It's going to be a little more approachable in its youth so you can drink it now.

Domaine Du Gros Nore Bandol

And a bonus Rosé recommendation.

Domaine Tempier Bandol Rosé

 Drink Well.

DRINKING & KNOWING THINGS
#20: BEAUJOLAIS

Ah, Burgundy. What is it about that place that inspires fanatical levels of devotion that culminate in special festivals where wine-crazed (sometimes tattooed) people gather together in special outfits over multiple days to revel in bacchanalian delight? I can wax poetically about Burgundy *ad infinitum*, but suffice it to say that Burgundy is the Harley-Davidson of the wine world, and the La Paulée event is the Sturgis. Different customer demographic, same maniacal passion for the product. Myself included.

While the Rockstar grapes of Burgundy are Pinot Noir and to a slightly lesser extent, Chardonnay, people forget that they do grow other grapes there. Some are relatively unknown grapes like Aligoté. However in the south of Burgundy in the region of Beaujolais, the Gamay grape reigns supreme.

Why Beaujolais is Dope AF:

When done right, Beaujolais is a light-bodied red wine, with soft tannins and juicy red fruit with spice and floral notes. It's low in alcohol (10-13%) so you can pound it all day. It can be similar to Burgundy, at a much lower price point. However, a lot of it is not done right and is nowhere near Dope AF. Which is why it has a bad rap.

Let's talk about volumes. By itself, the region of Beaujolais produces probably 40% of the entire volume of Burgundy. Size wise it is 45,000 acres, larger than Napa Valley. They make a shitload of volume.

A lot of it is bad.

Fortunately you all know the World's Leading Wine Influencer. Pay attention...

Why Beaujolais is Not Dope AF:

Somehow along the way, someone who wasn't into the whole "wait for the wine to age" thing had the bright idea of making what is called Beaujolais Nouveau. This is where they pick the grapes in September, make wine for six to eight weeks, and then release these wines the third Thursday in November. These wines cost $3-5 bucks. They can be best described as "youthful", although other adjectives may come to mind.

> **Side Note:** There is a funny story from the early 2000s where a French wine critic called Beaujolais Nouveau "vin merde" or "shit wine". The Beaujolais producers got together and sued him under some obscure French law that forbids talking shit (literally, in this case) on any French produced products. They won. So my attorney suggests that I add a legal caveat that all opinions presented herein are my own and may not represent the views of other people, notably Beaujolais Nouveau producers.

I've tried many times to like Beaujolais Nouveau, and I can't make it happen.

The next level of quality up from the Nouveau is labeled simply Beaujolais, and then slightly above that is labeled Beaujolais Villages. These are hit and miss depending on producer. Some are barely above the Nouveau quality level, and some are ambitious wines. Given the massive sprawl of producers here, I would caution purchasing these unless a specific bottle is recommended by someone who knows the producer and you trust.

> **Pro Tip:** If you do latch on to a producer of Beaujolais or Beaujolais Villages that you like, these wines can represent incredible values. You can get them for $15-20 all day long and some are eminently drinkable, particularly the ones labeled Beaujolais Villages.

The highest level of quality, where Beaujolais really shines, is called Cru Beaujolais. There are ten villages or "Crus" that make the very best Beaujolais. They are difficult to identify because nowhere on the label will you find the word "Beaujolais". This is a business strategy called "distancing your brand from the cheap crap".

Pro Tip: For the super geeky people, most of the bulk wine producers use a fermentation technique called carbonic maceration that produces a Hubba Bubba bubble gum flavor in the wine. Few of the Cru producers do it this way. Which I think contributes to the quality.

The Cru wines will be labeled with the name of the individual village they come from. Because of the terroir differences, some of the Cru villages produce a lighter, fruitier style. While these can be good, I prefer the darker, richer, spicier styles of Cru Beaujolais which are only made in four of the ten villages. Two of the villages are small and fairly tough to find. So we are going to make it easy for you and only concentrate on the other two villages.

These wines will be labeled either Morgon or Moulin-à-Vent.

Both of these villages produce a darker, fuller bodied style which is a) delicious and b) can actually age for fifteen to twenty years. In marked contrast to the Nouveau which has a shelf life of about six months at best.

Side Note: These wines IMHO represent some of the absolute best values in Burgundy. For $28-35 you can get a great Morgon or Moulin-à-Vent which will stand up against many Premier Cru Burgundy wines at $100+. In fact, it's an old MW exam trick to sneak a bottle of Cru Beaujolais into a Burgundy flight (because technically it is also from Burgundy) and see if people can differentiate it from the Pinot Noir. 60% of the time, I ace this every time.

Side Note +1: These wines used to be $20, until the Somm 2 movie came out and every single MS in it said the most underrated wine in the world was Beaujolais, and prices jumped 50% overnight in the opposite of what we call the "Sideways" effect. I wish they had talked shit – these wines might be $10 now.

Side Note +2: There are a couple of really kickass producers of Cru Beaujolais like Yvon Metras, whose wines are now selling for over $100 a bottle. I think is a harbinger of future price escalations to come. So please don't tell anyone about Beaujolais. Keep it our little secret.

On to our recommendations:

Given the choice, I am pretty much always going to opt for a Moulin-à-Vent, because they tend to be slightly richer on average than Morgon. At $30+, this one is a bit on the pricier side, because it is Albert Bichot who is one of the larger quality producers in Burgundy. You can find cheaper options from smaller independent producers, but Bichot is consistently solid.

Albert Bichot Moulin-à-Vent

And a Morgon. Get them both and try them against each other.

Dominique Piron Cote du Py Morgon

Pro Tip: serve it slightly chilled.

+1 Pro Tip: If you find you like wines a little more on the fruity side than the savory side, two Beaujolais Crus you can look out for will be labeled Fleurie or Saint Amour.

Drink Well!

DRINKING & KNOWING THINGS
#21: MADEIRA

You know how to make wine even better? Run it through a still and turn it into a 180-proof spirit like Brandy. Then dump the Brandy back into a bunch of wine during fermentation. The high alcohol will kill the yeast, leaving a wine that is super potent, but also sweet because there is a bunch of sugar left over that never got fermented.

This technique is used all over the world, to make a wide range of wines, from the rarest and most expensive Vintage Ports, to the cheapest plonk like Thunderbird.

If you're a Wineaux, you would call these wines "fortified", because you are classy. If you're a Wino, you would call these wines "breakfast".

I am a huge fan of fortified wines, and rest assured we are gonna cover a few different ones in the DAKT series. We are going to start with my favorite fortified wine, which is Madeira.

WTF is Madeira?

Madeira comes from a little island (called Madeira) a few hundred miles off the Northwest coast of Africa. Technically it is part of Portugal. The climate there is pretty inhospitable for growing grapes that make drinkable wine, so over the centuries they have evolved this technique to make the wines drinkable.

Side Note: One of the grapes there makes such shitty still wine that the name of it translates into "the dog strangler".

Here's how to make Madeira at home. Grab a bottle of white wine, pour it in a bucket and dump some vodka into it. Then stick the bucket in your attic or the trunk of your car or somewhere hot for ten years or longer until it turns dark brown. Voilà – Madeira! The key to making Madeira is lengthy periods of exposure to oxygen and heat. The two main things that we are normally warned against letting happen to our wines.

Sometimes, the higher volume producers don't want to wait ten years, and so instead they cook the wine – literally cook it – for at least ninety days. This simulates the ten-year attic waiting period.

Pro Tip: To cook the wine, they use a special heated wine tank called an "estufagem". Which is fun to say. Esss-toooo-Fa-gemmm. Use your best Ricardo Montalban voice.

Why Madeira is Dope AF:

First off, it's America's wine. Primarily because when we were fighting the Revolutionary War and were cut off from our European wine dealers, we could still score from Portugal. So that's what all the Founding Fathers drank. We celebrated signing the Declaration of Independence with Madeira.

If you don't drink Madeira then you are a flag-burning communist and quite possibly a terrorist. 'Murica, baby.

In addition to being America's wine, it is super delicious and an extraordinary value. There are two basic types of Madeira. Bulk, which is generally five years or fewer in age and is super cheap, usually under $15. Don't bother with these. And aged Madeira, which is older and more expensive. This is what we want. Preferably that which is at least ten or more years old.

They make aged Madeira from four different grapes, each of which results in different sweetness levels. They run the gamut from slightly sweet all the way up to very sweet. In all cases, the alcohol will be high, like 18-20% (bonus!).

Side Note: There are a couple of extra grapes that you might find in aged Madeira outside of the four main ones. You'll never run into these. I only mention it to preempt Erik from imperiously reminding me that Terrantez is also an allowable variety, even though it is almost extinct.

Because of the way Madeira is made it is bulletproof. This isn't a wine you need to worry about storing well. You can leave a glass of wine on the counter and come back a month later and it will taste exactly the same. You could leave a bottle in the trunk of your car for a year and it would be fine.

Because of the high alcohol it is hard to smash through a bottle of Madeira (well, it can be done, but it takes commitment). But because it is bulletproof, you can just have a glass now and then and not worry about it being open.

Flavor-wise, Madeira is going to be lots of leather, burnt orange peel, and candied almonds. Add high alcohol and sugar to the mix and you have yourself the perfect after dinner drink or cigar accompaniment.

Why I Really Love Madeira:

Madeira lasts forever. And is pretty cheap, relatively speaking, for older wine. It is easy to find bottles of fifty+ year old Madeira for a couple hundred bucks. Which is awesome. Imagine rolling into your next dinner party where everyone brought some cult 2015 Napa Cab, and you've got a 1947 Madeira tucked under your arm. Everyone will be like, fuck yeah I want to try that. And because it's bulletproof, you can pour everyone a glass and then leave the bottle uncorked for the next party three months later. In my experience, the older it is, the better it is.

Side Note: I have bought many bottles of aged Madeira and have never had a bad one. Recently I had a bottle of Madeira from 1840. This wine aged in a barrel for 110 years, and then another 70 years aging in the bottle. For the record, Martin Van Buren was President when this wine was made. How dope is that?

+1 Side Note: For the record that bottle was spectacular.

+2 Side Note: The older bottles often don't really have labels. Usually it is just a giant year painted on the side of the bottle. Which also makes it a great display item for the house. For a few hundred bucks you can buy a hundred-year-old bottle, and put it up on your bar and let your guests wonder what kind of person has hundred-year-old bottles of wine laying casually around their house. (A: the Dope AF kind, that's who...)

But you don't have to get the super old stuff to have fun with this. Here's some options:

This one is going to have the lowest level of sweetness:

The Rare Wine Co Historic Series Charleston Sercial

This will have the highest level of sweetness:

The Rare Wine Co Historic Series New York Malmsey

If you want to be dope, here's a fifty-year-old option:

D'Oliveira Bual Vintage Madeira 1968

And if you want to be as dope as me (like that's even possible):

D'Oliveira Verdelho Vintage Madeira 1850

Drink Well!

DRINKING & KNOWING THINGS
#22: NERELLO MASCALESE

If you've been carefully studying your DAKT, and trying new shit out, you are probably noticing a few things. You're probably spending a bit more time looking at the label and are starting to occasionally recognize and understand some of the weird things that are on it. Even the indecipherable European labels. You're starting to be far less intimidated by grapes you haven't heard of before. You're starting to trust your own palate more and more and are starting to become comfortable with deciding whether or not you like a particular wine, as opposed to relying on some insufferable wine "expert" to tell you whether a wine is "good" or not.

Congratulations. You're on your way to becoming the most knowledgeable (and insufferable) person about wine in your social circle, and being able to pull James Bond level stuff on somms.

There's still a lot of runway ahead though. Wine is ridiculously over complicated, and the wine market constantly evolves, with new styles and winemaking techniques coming in and out of fashion.

This is what keeps me interested in wine. That and the fact that it is an intoxicant.

Now, you also may be starting to pick up on the fact that Italy is a) one of the greatest countries for winemaking and b) stupidly complex. They have thousands of grapes that only grow in Italy, and they even have ten or more different names for the same grape. Then we also have the Italian nonchalance (which is French for "not giving a fuck") that allows them to treat the rules for things like labeling and winemaking as more of guidelines than hard and fast laws.

I think that is awesome. I love the wines of Italy and the fact that it is a completely unknowable wine region in its entirety makes it even better.

(For the record it also means you can't really be called out on any Italian wine fact, because there are always forty-two exceptions.)

Today we are going to head to Sicily and check out what's going on down there.

Why Sicilian Wine is Dope AF:

It isn't necessarily. Historically wines from Sicily have had a reputation for being cheap, high volume, and having "inconsistent" quality control. The main wine that built the Sicilian wine industry over the last couple of hundred years is Marsala. You know this as something to cook with, although I have heard that drinkable ones can be found (I have yet to find one btw). But the island has such a unique terroir, and such a rich history of winemaking that they can make some amazing wines. The terroir driven wines from Sicily have become an area of focus over the last few years. Generally speaking they represent great values as well.

> **Side Note:** Dionysus is credited with bringing grapes to Sicily. So it isn't just about the wine, it's about the whole party. If you have been to Sicily you know what I mean. If you haven't, well...that's on you.

What Sicilian Wines are Dope AF?

In my opinion, the most interesting Sicilian wines come from the vineyards on the slopes of Mount Etna. Which among other things is an active volcano, constantly belching smoke and occasionally erupting lava all over the vineyards. My favorite red wine from there is made from the Nerello Mascalese grape. These wines are sometimes labeled Nerello Mascalese, but more often than not they are labeled with the bland Etna Rosso designation (which means "red wine from Etna").

> **Side Note:** I am going to refer to Nerello Mascalese from here on out as "Nerello".

> **+1 Side Note:** I clarify this point in advance before Lyin' Bidet Yo informs me that they also make wine on Etna from Nerello Cappuccio.

+2 Side Note: A reasonable retort to this would be that Nerello Cappuccio is a far inferior grape, suitable only for blending, and that anyone who knows anything about wine knows this and therefore any winedouche worth his tannins knows that Nerello when used in conversation means Nerello Mascalese, in the same way that Cabernet means Cabernet Sauvignon and not Cabernet Franc, and that anyone who is nitpicky about that kind of stuff is either an asshole or from Philly or both. But because I am not a dick I won't make this retort.

Pro Tip: If you label the wine Etna Rosso, you can a) put the DOC label over the neck, which is a quality indicator and b) more importantly you can blend in up to 20% of the wine with about ten other grapes, some of which are white. This is important to know because some winemakers are choosing to go full on Nerello to showcase the beauty of that grape. Other winemakers want to create something special, so they mix in a little white wine to boost the aromatics, or a little wine from other red grapes to boost fruitiness or color or whatever. Then there is the unspoken third category in which the winemaker has a bit of cheaper other stuff left over so they dump it in the Nerello, which stretches the volume of that pricier wine.

But there's no way of knowing what the winemaker's strategy is unless you know them or have researched it. I try when possible to check the label and see if it is 100% Nerello or not. In true Italian nonchalance, sometimes they will put that on the label and sometimes not.

A price guide works pretty well here. If the wines are in the $15-25 range, they are most likely a blend. 100% Nerello wines are typically going to be in the $25-40 range, with a few standouts that are higher priced than that.

Flavor wise, Nerello is often compared to fine Pinot Noir. I personally don't think that is a fair comparison. It will have the fruitiness of Pinot, combined with rich smokiness and spice (growing on an active volcano will do that), and some herbal notes. And it will have high lean acidity. Where I think it differs from Pinot is that it is much more tannic. I think a better comparison is what you would get if you mixed Barolo and Burgundy together, and got the fruit from Burgundy and the tannin and acid from Barolo.

Side Note: I tried making a blend of Pinot Noir and Barolo a few years back. One of my many failed wine experiments. I still have a couple of cases of it laying down in the hopes that someday it might be good. Conceptually it totally makes sense to me. I want the fruit and I also want the structure. Nerello provides both.

Because Nerello has elevated tannin and acid, and also because it is from Italy where it is all about the food, these wines are amazing food wines. I think quite possibly the best wine pairing for lamb chops is Nerello.

Now, the recommendations:

I love these guys. They make a handful of wines. This is their entry level wine and great, but their single vineyard shit is amazing if you want to spend a few more bucks.

Tenuta delle Terre Nere Etna Rosso

Here's a super option from a top producer, with a price to match.

Pietradolce Vigna Barbagalli Etna Rosso

Drink Well!

Drinking & Knowing Things
#23: TOKAJI

Wine, like food, is ridiculously diverse. Saying you don't like wine is like saying you don't like food. It's absurd. You might say that you don't like specific foods, like broccoli, or specific food categories, like vegetables or red meat. But you would never say that you don't like food.

If you or someone you know falls into that category of people who continue to proclaim that they don't like wine, it is because they just haven't found their wine yet. If that's you, keep reading. If it is someone you know, stop hanging out with them immediately. You don't want that kind of negative energy in your life.

Imagine you are someone who likes refreshing zesty beverages like lemonade. If that is what your palate prefers, you will probably enjoy a wine like Albarino. Now imagine the first wine you ever try is a massive Australian Shiraz. You probably would then erroneously conclude that you don't like wine and are done with it. This is why we need to keep trying new wines.

Here's a story about a friend of mine. He would often tell me that he hated wine, for lots of different reasons. It gave him a headache. He didn't like the taste. The sun got in his eyes. Whatever. The point is that he was being a pussy about it. I kept telling him that he needed to keep trying until he found his wine.

This went on for years.

One night, we found ourselves in an extremely fancy (read: overpriced) restaurant in San Francisco, where they were doing *prix fixe* tasting menus, with an optional wine pairing. I of course immediately opted in for the wine pairing and started having uber-winedouche conversations with the sommelier, who recognized me as one of his own, and started bringing things that were not on the menu over to see what I thought about them.

I offered a taste of one of the wines he shared with me to my friend, who initially shook it off, until I pleasantly reminded him that he hadn't yet found his wine (technically I berated him incessantly in front of all our friends for being a monumental Sissy La La). He grudgingly tried a sip and immediately lost his mind, and began effusively expressing that it was a) awesome, b) he finally got what the wine hype was all about and c) could I have some more please. (I said no, for the record. Fuck him.)

We call these wines epiphany wines. Hopefully you have had, or will have, a handful of these wine moments in your life where everything aligns perfectly and you remember it forever.

This is the story of that particular wine, which is called Tokaji.

Why Tokaji is Dope AF:

Everything about this wine is atypical. Let's start with the fact that it is made in Hungary, a country that you normally won't see on a list of kickass wine countries. Next, it's made primarily from the Furmint and Harslevelu grapes (yep, I never heard of them before either). Lastly, it is made from the grapes that have rotted on the vine.

Rotten grapes from varieties you never heard of, from a country not known for wine. What's not to love?

But it makes a spectacular dessert wine. The wines are syrupy sweet, but with fresh acidity that balances out the sweetness. Flavor wise you will get notes of saffron, ginger, honey and crème brulee.

Pro Tip: It's pronounced Toe-Kai. Although there is some debate with the Wineauxs about whether it is also pronounced Toe-Kay or Toe-Coy. Since I am not Hungarian I have no real clue on this one. Probably all three are wrong and only used by dumb Americans who can't make guttural loogie sounds in the back of their throat whilst pronouncing a word. But I have said Toe-Kai for years without any problems, so as the World's Leading Wine Influencer I hereby issue an edict that going forward it will always be Toe-Kai.

Let's lean in a bit on the whole "rotten grapes" thing. While this sounds terrible, botrytis or "noble rot" infection is how the best dessert wines around the world are made. You wait until the botrytis sucks the water out of the grapes, and then press the remaining sugar out of the shriveled little grapes and it makes a beautiful sweet wine.

Pro Tip: This is exactly how the very pricey wines of Sauternes are made. Also that Egon Muller baller wine from the Riesling DAKT. But Tokaji is one-third the price of the equivalent Sauternes. And one-three hundredth the price of the Muller.

+1 Pro Tip: The rot affects grape bunches inconsistently, so the most selective wineries make a number of trips through the vineyard hand-selecting the rotten berries one at a time. And you thought your job was rough...

+2 Pro Tip: This hand picking one berry at a time, plus the fact that you lose 70% of your volume due to water loss means that these wines are ridiculously time consuming and costly to make. Which is why most of them around the world are quite expensive. While Tokaji isn't cheap per se (usually $40-60), it is super cheap compared to other botrytized wines.

+3 Pro Tip: Asking a somm if a sweet wine is "botrytized" is instant street cred. Unless it's a red wine. Then you are an asshole.

There are three sweetness levels of Tokaji. They will indicate this on the label as either "five puttonyos", "six puttonyos" or "Eszencia".

Pro Tip: Before 2013 they also allowed three and four puttonyos versions so you might see those on older bottles.

A puttonyo is a measure of sweetness. Five is pretty sweet. Six is even sweeter. The Eszencia (or Essencia as it is sometimes spelled) is a delight – it is like three times as sweet as the six puttonyos. It looks and pours like honey. If you can get your hands on some of this you should absolutely try it at least once in your life.

Side Note: The mind-blowing wine in the story above was an Eszencia.

Now the recommendations!

Five and six puttonyos are pretty equivalent in my mind – so I usually look to vintage more than puttonyos levels. The older the better. We want a minimum of ten years if possible. Often you may see the word Aszú on the label as well – which basically is Hungarian for "rotten grapes".

Here's a kickass five puttonyos. This should be drinking extremely nicely right now.

Royal Tokaji Five Puttonyos

Seriously buy this right now and have it for dessert this weekend.

Now the baller selection. Like most baller wines, the Eszencia is a bitch to get your hands on. Supply and distribution in the US are super limited. But here's an option.

Pajzos Essencia

Final Pro Tip: Legally in a lot of countries Eszencia can't even be called wine because the alcohol is too low (and the sugar is too high). Back in the day it used to be sold in pharmacies. I think this means it qualifies as medicine.

Drink Well!

And take your medicine...

Drinking & Knowing Things

#24: RIOJA

If you like oaky wines then you are an asshole and an idiot.

Yep, I said that. Let the social media shitstorm begin...

Let's talk about what oak adds to wine. It's pretty simple. Aging in oak:

Allows the wine to soften and the elements to harmonize and integrate.

Imparts oak flavors to the wine (particularly when newer barrels are used).

Imparts oak tannins to the wine. (Not helpful in white wines.)

None of these things appear on the surface to be a bad thing. Why then is oak such a polarizing topic?

I think a good analogue for oak is salt. Most food dishes benefit from salt. In fact, I don't want to ever eat certain dishes unless they are salted (like steak). But I don't want the dishes to ever taste salty. I would never take a big bite of ribeye where all I could taste was salt and proudly exclaim "Damn, this steak is good. It's so salty. Here, smell the salt. Wow!"

But somehow this has become the norm for many types of wine. Napa of course is probably the biggest offender, but Australia and Chile are right up there as well. In fact, oaky wines have become so commonplace that many winemakers just dump oak chips or sawdust into the wine so it tastes more "oaky". This does literally nothing for the quality of the wine, except maybe adding in some more tannins.

How did this horrific travesty occur? Well, certain high-end wines (let's call them "Bordeaux") had a longstanding reputation for being high in quality. These wines need years of aging. Hitting them with a ton of new French oak gives them the structure to age gracefully, and if you wait fifteen or twenty years they are magnificent.

Except we are humans, and we want instant gratification, so we drink them now. And they taste super oaky. Because we "know" that these wines are high in quality, we now associate the taste of oak with high quality. And voilà, we get assholes dumping sawdust into huge vats of cheap shitty wine to make them taste expensive.

Side Note: Some critics (let's call them "Robert Parker") gave the highest ratings to these big oaky wines, which only further exacerbated the situation. Then these wines commanded a higher price point because they were ninety-five points or whatever, so everyone else started turning the oak up to eleven. The invisible hand works...

+1 Side Note: A new French oak barrel costs about $1500 and holds three hundred bottles of wine. So if you want 100% new barrel aging on your wine, your cost as the winemaker increases by $5 per bottle. By the time that added cost passes through distributors and retailers and everyone takes margin, you as the end consumer end up paying an extra $40 for that wine, which is now oaked to death.

+2 Side Note: Imagine going to Morton's and they were like, "Yo we got this tasty ribeye for $50, but if you want us to salt it to the point of unrecognizability as beef, we also have that option for $100". You would walk out.

This would be much less of a problem if we waited twenty years. But we won't.

Why Oaky Wines are Dope AF:
They're not. Stop buying them. You're part of the problem.

That said, I firmly believe that oak has a major role in winemaking, when done right. What we need to do is explore how oak is used to be accretive to the quality of the wine. This is gonna be our experiment for this week. For this little exercise we are going to go to Spain, to a region you may have heard of called Rioja.

Why Rioja is Dope AF:

In Rioja, they basically make three levels of quality wine, primarily from the Tempranillo grape. Crianza, Reserva, and Gran Reserva. A major difference between these wines is the use of oak. The minimum aging for Crianza is two years (one must be in oak), minimum for Reserva is three years, and Gran Reserva is five. They also often use higher percentages of newer barrels for the Reserva and Gran Reserva wines.

Pro Tip: A barrel will give the most oak flavor in the first year, followed by less flavor in the second year and a little bit in the third year. After that you will still get the aging benefit, but not really any oak flavors.

This is an awesome experiment which works best if you open these wines all at the same time and taste them against each other. It will really help you understand how oak works in the development of wine. (Plus you get to drink three bottles. Bonus!)

Here are three from the same winemaker.

Bodegas Faustino Crianza

Bodegas Faustino Reserva

Bodegas Faustino Gran Reserva

Side Note: one of the things I really like about Faustino is that they ignore the minimums and wait until they believe the wine is ready to drink. They typically age the Gran Reserva for ten years or more before releasing them.

Pro Tip: I think Gran Reserva Rioja may be the best value for dollar of any wine if you appreciate aged wines. Super easy to find thirty-year-old bottles for $50.

Open all three wines and pour a glass of each. They will all be great, but very different from one another (even though it's basically the same grapes from the same vineyards). Smell across the three glasses. Look at the color. Try mixing them up and see if you can figure out which is the youngest and which is the oldest just by the smell.

Now start drinking them!

The Crianza is likely to be fruity and fresh, with some hints of oak. But that oak will be newer and fresher smelling and less integrated into the wine. The Reserva is going to have more oak aging, but note that the wine will taste much more integrated. Then the Gran Reserva is going to be a whole different experience. Rather than fruity flavors, you should get more cigar and earthiness and leather. You will be able to note the seamless integration of all the elements, rather than silos of flavor and texture.

Hopefully this will allow you to start to hone your palate around what oak smells like and how it impacts the wine. If you want to do a really cool follow up to this experiment, go to your local wine store and buy any bottle of Cabernet Sauvignon that is under $15. With 99% certainty, this wine is going to be overoaked with the use of staves or chips. Then drink it, preferably against the Gran Reserva. You will note that the Cabernet smells and tastes imbalanced, and you will likely find that the tannins in your cheeks feel grainy and harsh.

Then pour the rest of the Cabernet down the sink and don't do that again.

Drink Well!

DRINKING & KNOWING THINGS
#25: WTF IS A TANNIN - PART 1

We Wineauxs have developed this whole intricate language around talking about wine. While it can be super fun to completely geek out about wine with your friends, inevitably these discussions can devolve into these whole dick measuring contests around who knows the most about wine and who knows the most words. You all know exactly what I am talking about, especially if you have been unfortunate to have been around me and Erik or Ryan blind tasting. And I bet that sometimes you have stood there listening to one of these conversations thinking "I have no idea what he/she is talking about." Then you feel like an idiot, and conclude that you don't want to have any part of this whole wine thing. It's too intimidating, and requires too much effort.

This is where I come in. If you pay attention to me, all you will have to do is invest ten minutes a week reading (in order to Know Things) and then smash through a bunch of wine. I have distilled everything worth knowing down to the point where it is completely assimilable by anyone, even you State School kids. Within a matter of weeks you will start to operate at a higher wine game than most of the people you know. Except me of course. Let's not get crazy...

Anyway, there's a ton of wine jargon. I am going to separate these into three major categories.

Shit that is important and actually matters and is good for you to know. Smart wine people use these all the time and they are meaningful. Example: acidity, as in "this wine has bracing acidity".

Shit that is completely unimportant, that people don't really understand and only use to make other douchebags believe they are important. Example: robust, as in "this wine is really robust" (or "precocious" or "insouciant" or pick your dumb adjective). Side Note: sometimes I will go all in on using these when I'm talking to some really annoying arrogant wine snob to watch them fumble around trying to respond.

Shit that is so technical that only the geekiest of wine geeks care about them, but they care so much that you can take multi-day training courses in that one tiny thing. Like "osmotic flow".

Tannins are interesting because they fall into all three categories.

Fortunately you all have access to the World's Leading Wine Influencer, so follow my guidance my young Padowans and you too will be able to winedouche with the best of them.

So WTF is a Tannin?

We don't really know 100% exactly how tannins work. But we have some ideas. About every eighteen months some new wine scientist issues a new paper about how they have cracked the code. And that is the current thinking until the next paper. Ask five winemakers about tannins and you will get seven different explanations.

I'm gonna try to make it easy for you.

Tannins are things that plants produce so that animals won't eat them.

It's a survival mechanism. They taste bitter. Don't believe me? Go outside and pick up a blade of grass or a piece of bark off a tree or a stalk of a flower. Now chew on it.

Bitter, right?

Yep, that's tannins. In wine, tannins manifest in the skins of the grapes. The skins are heavy with tannins, more so in particular varieties. This protects the seed from birds eating it until the seed is big enough to reproduce. Eventually the berry ripens and turns sweet, and the bird tolerates the bitterness of the skin long enough to get to the sweet part, and they eat the grape and then shit out the seed somewhere else while they're flying around and procreation occurs. (Feel free to pause a moment and hum the Circle of Life from the Lion King.)

We want tannins in red wines. When we make red wine, we mash up the grape skins with the juice and let it sit, sometimes for weeks, letting the wine steep in the skins, like an overused tea bag, extracting tannins until we get the style of wine we want. For white wines we get the skins away from the juice as soon as possible so as to not fuck it up with tannins. Unless we are hipsters and/or natural winemakers at which point all bets are off for white wines.

Pro Tip: Some winemakers really want tannins, so instead of letting the wine sit on the skins, they stir up the skins and mash them around and pump the wine up and back over the skins for days or weeks, like when you try to make tea steep more quickly by dunking the tea bag up and down an bunch of times and smushing it with your spoon to squeeze out more tea.

+1 Pro Tip: You know what else is a plant? An oak tree. So there's tannins in oak barrels as well. When you age wine in oak, those tannins go into the wine too. And sometimes these tannins connect to the wine tannins and then you get a wine that has grape tannins, oak tannins and hybrid chains of grape and oak tannins.

+2 Pro Tip: Tannins drift around and occasionally bump into one another and connect together. Over time these chains get longer. Once they get too heavy to float, they sink to the bottom of the bottle. That's what most of the black crap at the bottom of wines is, especially older wines. What we commonly call "sediment".

Why do we want tannins in red wines?

Tannins do a number of things. They provide the backbone to allow a wine to age. Tannins like to attach themselves at a molecular level to proteins, which is why a) red wines are good with steak and b) why you feel the tannins in your cheeks and gums (because those are also made of protein). There are many opinions about tannins and the appropriate amount in a wine. I think it is all about balance. You don't want the wine to be too tannic at the expense of everything else that is going on. Or not tannic enough to support the body of the wine.

Also, remember that tannins are going to help support the aging process of a wine. If you want to make a big extracted red wine that can age for twenty years or more, you want there to be a lot of tannins. You're going to do this by using all the tricks in your winemaking bag: smashing down the skins every couple of hours, letting the wine sit on the skins for weeks, using new oak barrels and letting the wine age in them for a couple years. At the end of all of this you will have a wine that has very high levels of tannins, and can age for years.

Except we drink them immediately. And we end up with a super tannic wine. And we wonder why.

Pro Tip: There are certain wines that are naturally very tannic, like Barolo. I have a rule that I won't drink a Barolo unless it is at least seven years old. Because I know it will be too tannic for my preference.

Side Note: We all have that friend who says they can't drink red wine because it gives them a headache. Morons blame this on sulfites. (More on this later – there's a rant brewing...) What I think however is that some people have a heightened allergic response to tannins and this is what causes those headaches. If that is you, try drinking some red wines that are low in tannins (like Beaujolais Villages) and see if that changes things for you.

Tannins, like women, are one of those things that get increasingly more unknowably complex the more you try to understand them. We're gonna do the master class next week, but this week is just about understanding how tannins work in your mouth. Imagine steeping a tea bag for two days, and then drinking that tea. It would be astringent and bitter in your mouth, almost puckering.

Wine is going to work the same way. The tannins will attach to your cheeks and gums and will feel rough and drying.

Here's the easiest way to understand what tannins are, and isolate them in the glass. For this experiment you will need a bottle of Pinot Noir and a bottle of Cabernet Sauvignon. Get it from anywhere, any producer, any price.

Open both up and pour a glass of each.

Don't bother smelling the wine or swirling it and don't pay any attention to the fruit flavors or aromas. Frankly, feel free to hold your nose shut if you want – it will work even better. Start with the Pinot and take a large mouthful. Swish it around like mouthwash for at least thirty seconds. Then swallow it. Waste not, want not...

Now pay attention to how your cheeks and gums feel. You probably will not get much drying or roughness. You probably won't pucker your lips. You might get a small sensation.

Repeat the process with the Cab.

It should become immediately apparent what tannins are. You will feel roughness and drying all around your cheeks and perhaps your gums as well.

Side Note: With Cabernet you generally won't feel any tannins on your tongue. This is why people sometimes refer to the "hole in the middle" with Cabernet tannins. You feel them all around the sides of your mouth but not in the middle.

And that's a kickass segue into next week's master class on tannins. Now that you have the basics down, I'll show you some next level tannins game.

Drink Well!

Drinking & Knowing Things

#26: WTF IS A TANNIN, PART DEUX

In today's masterclass, we are gonna elevate your tannins game to a whole new level. This is the kind of stuff that very few people know how to do, but it is way easier than you would think. It just requires a slightly different mindset and a little practice.

The major issue that I see with most people when they talk about tannins is that they focus on only one aspect – which is the overall quantity of the tannins.

Maybe a good analogue for this is thinking about spice in food. The quantity of the spice is important, sure. One dish is two stars spicy and another one is four stars. Or peppers, or little emojis with smoke coming out the ears or whatever.

But this completely ignores the nature of the spice. Atomic buffalo wings and red curry plates and salsa can all be super spicy but the spice itself is very different. The flavors, textures, length of finish etc all vary – although each dish is "hot".

We want to think about tannins in the same way. The quantity is important, but let's not forget that the quantity is a major function of age. Tannins soften and diminish over time. In my opinion, the nature of the tannins is way more important. Frankly when I am blind tasting a red wine, the nature of the tannins is one of the major things I focus on, far more than the quantity of tannins.

Let's start by saying that all grape varieties have different tannin structures. We have no idea how or why this works, but it is the case.

Cabernet is different than Syrah, which is different than Pinot etc. Also one thing I have noticed is that different people experience tannins from the same grape differently. So there isn't a hard fast rule on these. It really comes down to you paying attention to the tannins and then honing in your experience with them.

Pro Tip: Since everyone is going to experience tannins a little differently this also means your opinion on them can never be wrong.

The first thing we want to focus on is where in your mouth do you experience the tannins. As mentioned before this will vary between different grape varieties. For this lesson, you will need a bottle of Syrah. Any will do, but if you can grab an Australian Shiraz that would be preferable. Pour a glass, hold your nose, take a big mouthful and swish it around for a bit. Swallow it and now pay attention to where you feel the dryness/roughness in your mouth.

For me with Shiraz I almost exclusively feel this on the inside of my upper lip. It feels like I grew a thick moustache on the inside, and I feel it almost nowhere else in my mouth. However, a good MW friend of mine always talks about how one of his tells for Syrah is he feels the tannins across the middle of his tongue. Who's right? Me, of course. Fuck that guy.

No, not really. The point that no one is right. It's is merely a sense of dialing in how you experience tannins with different wines. Going forward, start paying attention to where you feel the tannins. If you happen to have a bottle of something else open, try the experiment again right now and I bet you will feel the tannins in a different area.

The next aspect we are going to focus on is the texture of the tannins. Think about the bark of a redwood tree, very coarse, versus the bark of a birch tree, very smooth. Both are trees, both have tannins, but the texture is quite different. If you chewed pieces of the bark from these trees both would be bitter, but you would have a very different textural experience. Same with wine. A way to think about this is how the tannins feel against your cheeks, lips, etc. Do they feel like rough sandpaper? Or do they feel almost silky and supple? Are they gritty and large grained like rice or fine like pieces of sand?

Feel free to keep going with your Shiraz for this. Take another large mouthful and swish. This time don't worry about where you feel them, try to focus on feeling the texture. For me, Shiraz has a medium rough texture, like mid-grade sandpaper. A great comparison for this is Grenache, or Garnacha as they call it in Spain. Grab a bottle of Grenache and repeat the experiment. For me Grenache has very soft tannins. Almost like someone was rubbing the inside of my cheeks, but with a piece of silk rather than a piece of linen (Syrah) or a piece of burlap (Tannat).

> **Pro Tip:** Tannins accumulate in your mouth. If you drink a very tannic wine, like Barolo and then immediately drink a lower tannin wine, like Pinot Noir, the Pinot will taste more tannic than it actually is. So when you are doing the experiment above, you should actually start with the Grenache instead of the Syrah. Apologies to those of you who are playing along at home as you read. One of these days I will actually bother to outline these DAKTs in advance rather than just riffing.

Who are we kidding? I'm way too lazy to do that.

The next thing I think about is the timeline of the tannins. How soon do you feel the tannins? Do they attack your cheeks the second you drink the wine, or do they come in on the back end after you swallow? How long does the feeling remain in your mouth? Hit that Shiraz again, but this time pay attention to when the feeling starts and stops. Is it gone in five seconds or does it linger for a minute or longer? And pay attention to the arc of it. Does it continue to build, or does it hit hard and fast before dropping away quickly?

I also think about the ripeness of the tannins. This is a bit more esoteric, and harder to explain. But some tannins will have a greenness, almost underripe character to them, while others seem more almost dried in character. Take another refreshing gulp of that Shiraz and see if you come to any conclusions about it. If not, no big deal. This nuance can take a while to dial in, and frankly I'm not convinced that I'm even that good at consistently identifying it.

The last thing, and perhaps one of the most important for me when enjoying a wine, is the level of integration of the tannins into the wine as a whole. When you drink the wine, do the tannins stand out as their own thing? Or are they just a seamless part of the wine? We want complex wines that are interesting, but we want them to be well balanced. I don't want any one element, whether it be fruit, or tannin, or acid, or alcohol (or God forbid, oak) to be dominant. This is a function of how high quality and how old your wine is – so there won't be one answer for everyone. But drink your Shiraz again and see if you have an opinion about how integrated and balanced the tannins are with the wine, or if they stand out as their own separate thing.

Side Note: Trying to find that perfect balance is why age is so important. A monster of a Bordeaux is gonna be way too tannic if the wine is five years old, but if you wait fifty years it will probably go the other way. Somewhere in the middle is the sweet spot, but it is a crap shoot and you won't know if you hit it or not until the bottle is open.

+1 Side Note: A Bordeaux winemaker once told me the trick to buying Bordeaux is to always buy three cases of the current release. Then in about six or seven years, start opening one bottle every year to see how it is aging. When it gets to that sweet spot, immediately have all your friends over and drink the whole second case. Then you sell the third case, which by now is worth more money and you break even on the whole deal.

+2 Side Note: A great time to start doing that is fifteen years ago. Starting now you're just gonna be sitting on inventory for years.

So that's it. The tannins master class done. You are now able to play in the wine big leagues. The next time some tool is loudly espousing how tannic a wine is, feel free to respond with something like "Yeah, it's pretty tannic, but the tannins are fine-grained and silky and well integrated. You can really feel them across the back of your cheeks, and they linger on the finish."

Pro Tip: Remember, you don't have to be accurate with any of this shit, because there is no way to prove that you didn't experience the tannins that way!

Then lean back and smile while attractive people hurl themselves at you as the most interesting wine person in the room.

(Enjoy that while you can. Trust me, it gets extremely old after a while...)

And remember to Drink Well!!

DRINKING & KNOWING THINGS
#27: ARNEIS

Anyone who is into wine (myself included), even if they aren't geeky and/or snobby about it (myself excluded), has at least one and maybe more stories about what turned them on to wine. I love hearing these. Usually the stories involve more than just the wine and involve the whole experience, where people were, what they were doing and and who they were with.

Recently, I was hanging with Kit and he told the story around how he and Mrs. Kit got turned on to white wine. As is typical, the story was about a special place and family and good times. The specific wine they drank stuck with him to this day. This is the story of that particular wine, called Arneis, which I am an enormous fan of. As he was telling the story, I was like damn, I need to inform the DAKT crew about the delicious goodness that is Arneis.

Arneis is from Piedmont, Italy. In my opinion, Piedmont is hands down the best wine region in the world.

Yes, I am aware that some of you Burgundyphiles are prepared to burn me at the stake or stone me to death for heresy when I make that statement. But hear me out.

Why Piedmont is Dope AF:
Piedmont is awesome because the people there take wine making seriously and take wine drinking as fun. The range of wines is super broad. They make big reds, Barolo and Barbaresco. They make light fruity fun sparkling Moscato, and rich traditional Champagne style sparkling wines in Alta Langa. They make easy drinking fruity reds, like Dolcetto and the more powerful Barbera. They make sweet wines like Brachetto d'Acqui and aromatized wines like Chinato. And they make a ton of delicious white

wines, from more well-known grapes like Arneis or Cortese, and lesser known grapes like Timorasso. All of them are Dope, and many rise to the Dope AF benchmark that we care about. Except Moscato. Fuck Moscato.

Plus, they also produce a lot of dried pig products and truffles. Which I know isn't wine but is totally worthy of a mention in the Why Piedmont is Dope AF category.

I know of no other wine region with the variety and range of high-quality wines than Piedmont. If I was stranded on a deserted island, and was allowed to take one thing with me, it would be the entire Piedmont region. And a Costco. It better be a big island...

Why Arneis is Dope AF:

Now, back to where all this started, with Arneis. This grape has been cultivated in Piedmont for hundreds of years, but over time, the focus on it has waned a bit. Primarily because you can tear it out and replant it with Nebbiolo, which has a much higher price point. Also Arneis is temperamental and a bitch to grow. Its name translates as "little rascal".

Historically, this grape was used to blend in with Nebbiolo to soften the tannins. This is why you will hear it sometimes referred to as Barolo Bianco, or "white Barolo". We haven't needed this as much lately, as Barolo producers have started using a variety of modern winemaking techniques to make a more approachable style of Barolo that doesn't need to be softened. Consequently, more Arneis is available to bottle as a single variety wine.

Side Note: There is a huge conflict raging in Piedmont about whether or not these newer methods of winemaking improve and advance Barolo, or whether they are a completely bastardization of the traditional processes that made Barolo what it is today. And when I say conflict I mean people (and by people I mean passionate high spirited Italian people) have extremely strong opinions on the topic one way or another and have been fighting like rabid wolverines about it for the last thirty years. It's like the Italian version of the Hatfields vs the McCoys. There's a cool documentary on Netflix called Barolo Boys that is worth a watch, if you are interested in this level of geekdom.

+1 Side Note: As the World's Leading Wine Influencer I probably should have an opinion on that debate, but I don't. I think it is great to have more modern styles that you can drink when they are younger, and more traditional styles that don't start getting interesting until they are ten years old. I see a place in the world for both to co-exist. Primarily in my stomach.

Many Italian white wines, particularly those grown in the cooler Northern parts, are relatively homogeneous and uninteresting. They all have high bracing acidity, medium body at best, and often have more minerality than fruit. They can kind of blur together, especially the cheaper high-volume wines. Not so much with Arneis though. It generally is fairly full bodied, with rich ripe tropical fruit notes. The acidity, while elevated, isn't face ripping, and the alcohol is usually in the 13% range or slightly higher.

If you get this much tropical fruit from Arneis in a cooler climate, it makes me wonder what type of fruit profile we would get if we started making Arneis in warmer New World climates and styles. They have planted it in Cali, Australia and New Zealand, although I confess I haven't tried any of these because I am a Piedmont snob. I'm curious though.

But there is no need to look for alternatives. Arneis from Piedmont is a great white wine, at a value driven price point. If you like unoaked Sonoma Chardonnay, you'll probably love this wine, and so will your pocketbook.

There are two specific areas that specialize in Arneis. One is Roero, and the other is Langhe. Generally, these will be labeled as "Roero Arneis" or "Langhe Arneis". That said, I have also seen bottles that were simply labelled Arneis, or simply Roero.

Side Note: I really like Arneis from Roero, so a while back I bought a case from one of my wine connections. Great price, like $13 a bottle. Laid it down to let it age a few months and then cracked one open. Imagine my surprise when I tipped the dark green bottle over my glass and watched red wine pour out of it. This is how I learned that they also label Nebbiolo and some other red grapes as simply "Roero" as well. So be careful out there.

+1 Side Note: After the shock of that event wore off, and I tasted the wine, I realized that I had actually bought a case of ridiculously good Nebbiolo for $13 a bottle. Which made everything ok. I'll take that deal any time.

On to our recommendations:

The first is from Vietti – and we gotta represent for these guys. In the 1970s, Arneis had dwindled so much it was on the verge of extinction, and Vietti was one of only two producers that kept it going. Mad respect.

Vietti Roero Arneis

And here's one from a newer producer.

Michele Chiarlo Arneis

Lastly, for those feeling adventurious (that's adventurous and curious) – here's a New World one from a famous Sonoma Zinfandel producer. Caveat – I have no idea if this is good or not. I fear it could be way overextracted and overripe. But an interesting experiment. I'm gonna pick some of this up just to see what's up.

Seghesio Arneis

Drink Well!

DRINKING & KNOWING THINGS
#28: CORVINA

If you are a baller like me or Clooney, and spend your free time hanging around Lake Como with supermodels, Corvina needs no introduction. But for the rest of you poor slobs who live uneventful lives and whose sole moment of joy is when your email dings with another DAKT email and you get the opportunity to live vicariously through the eyes of the World's Leading Wine Influencer, I recognize that Corvina is gonna need a bit of a back story.

Also, there's different versions of these wines, which make things more difficult. I will break this down for you and tell you what you need to know.

First off, the Corvina grape is grown almost exclusively in the Veneto region of Italy – between Venice and Lake Garda, just east of Lake Como. No other global wine region has figured out how to make it work effectively there. The Italians have a hammerlock on the Corvina game.

In the Veneto, they make a handful of different wines based primarily on the Corvina grape. Historically, these were blends, where the winemakers would mix in a bit of Rondinella or Molinara or maybe some other local reds. We are seeing a lot less of that these days though, with many winemakers opting for single variety wine, or close enough to single variety that the blend isn't worth mentioning.

Why Corvina is Dope AF:

That's an interesting question. I am not necessarily convinced that Corvina is Dope AF. But I am convinced that it can be Dope AF. They produce a shit ton of volume there. Probably second to only Chianti in Italy in terms of liters made annually. Generally speaking these wines are labeled Valpolicella. Sometimes you will see them also labeled Bardolino.

On its own, Corvina is a light, fruity wine. It reminds me a lot of Beaujolais. Not Cru Beaujolais, just everyday run of the mill Beaujolais. Which is fine; it means you can get a super easy to drink picnic wine for like $8-12 bucks that won't be offensive to anyone.

But not necessarily Dope AF, except the price.

They also make a special version of this wine, which will be labeled Amarone. They do this by drying out the grapes for a few months until they are super raisinated, and then crush and ferment them. Since a lot of the water is gone from the grapes, you get a much more concentrated wine. And by concentrated I mean it smells and tastes like raisins, and is also 16+% alcohol. I definitely like me some Amarone, but I have to be in the right mood. Plus they can be pricey, and are too aggressive when they are young. But worth checking out.

When you peel back the layers of Corvina, some other interesting options come to light. The first is a Superiore version of the basic Valpolicella. Like other areas in Italy, the Superiore means that the alcohol has a higher minimum requirement and there is more aging required. So the winemakers are going to use their best and ripest grapes for the wines labeled Valpolicella Superiore. These wines are a bit more robust and complex, and the price point doesn't move up a lot – maybe up to $10-15 a bottle. These are great little options – trending towards Dope AF, but not quite there yet.

Here's where shit gets interesting. Sometimes, they take the leftover raisin skins from making Amarone, and they dump these into their Superiore wine and let it sit on those skins for a while. Now we have the highest level quality Corvina grapes, and we add in a bunch of complexity to the wine by adding in some raisinated grape skins. This is going to make the wine more aromatic, add in some notes of fig and spice, and make the body fuller without making it too over the top. This is called Valpolicella Ripasso.

I will admit that this style likely came about by thrifty Italian winemakers who were like "Yo, we got these skins left over, what else can we use them for?" In this case, however, the process actually worked and made the wines better. In marked contrast to the undrinkable paint thinner that is called Grappa, also made from leftover grape skins.

There's one additional style I would be remiss if I didn't mention, which is labeled Recioto della Valpolicella. This is a sweet wine. They make it basically the same way that the make Amarone, but they don't let the wine ferment all the way to dryness. It's sweet, but also raisiney. (Raisin-ish? Raisin-esque? Not sure on the right adjective to use there.)

Some people love this wine. I'm kind of meh on it. I'd rather have a Vin Santo if I was having an Italian dessert wine. But it isn't awful. The main reason I mention it is because one of you chumps (likely Clayton) will be at Trader Joe's and will see a bottle that has the word Valpolicella on the label, and will buy it and then be like, hey man this wine is sweet. And then will unjustly determine that Valpolicella isn't for them, when in fact they just grabbed the wrong bottle. So be careful out there.

In summary, if the label says:
Valpolicella – buy for picnics.

Valpolicella Superiore – buy for higher end picnics.

Amarone – save for special occasions requiring a big wine, or times when you want to get hammered quickly, like before church or dinner with your in-laws.

Recioto della Valpolicella – don't go out of your way, but drink it if someone gives you a glass.

Valpolicella Ripasso – yeah, get after this!

I'm only gonna provide Ripasso recommendations, but feel free to play around with the others.

This one is on the bigger side.

Rocca Sveva Valpolicella Ripasso

This one is on the spicier side.

Tommasi Valpolicella Ripasso

Note – most Ripasso wines are gonna be in the $20-30 range which make them great values in my mind.

Drink Well!

Drinking & Knowing Things
#29: TOURIGA NACIONAL

I love it when I find some fantastic wine that no one knows about. You get this amazing wine which typically has a unique style or flavor profile that is unique to where it is from, and the wines are $20 or less. When I find these, I load up on them. First, I like drinking interesting wines, and I also like not paying a bunch of money for them. Secondly, it's always great when I roll into a party where everyone brought the same old Napa Chardonnays and Oregon Pinots, and I throw down some Mondeuse, or Picpoul or Nerello or whatever and everyone loses their shit, because it is a) good and b) interesting.

> **Side Note:** when that happens there's always that one person who goes "ewww, this is too earthy or fruity or too delicious" and then they go back to their Rombauer. You know the person I am talking about. You might even be married to this person, Chuck.

Don't be that person!

I am always highly annoyed when I find something amazing, and then somehow it gets blown up in the media, and then everyone wants it, and the prices go up, and worse, every producer in that area starts pumping out as much volume as they can and the quality goes down.

This happened to Portugal.

Time for a history lesson. This isn't all about drinking, you know. Sometimes we gotta know things too, in order to justify our monthly wine expenditures. (I'm studying...it's necessary...)

Now, in Portugal, they've been making all kinds of Port since basically forever. Tawny, ruby, vintage, Colheita – the list goes on and on. We'll definitely get to a Port DAKT at some point, because it is awesome. Not today though. Today we are going to focus on still wines, and particularly red still wines.

Pro Tip: Portugal has some ridiculous wine laws. I mean, the US has antiquated and stupid wine laws, but Portugal adds an absurd layer of complexity on top. Every single vineyard is measured and given points on fourteen different dimensions, from criteria like how old the vines are to what specific grapes are planted to how much granite is in the soil. Then the points are added up and the total score is used to determine an overall vineyard grade from A-F. This grade then dictates things like how much the grapes should sell for, and also how many grapes can be harvested (higher quality vineyards are allowed to harvest more grapes which means more wine and therefore more money).

Side Note: this system, called Quinta, dates back to the 18th century, when it was probably needed to guarantee quality. Now I think it is more about control.

Next, we have to understand the Port quota process, called Beneficio. This is essentially a license granted to a particular producer to produce a certain volume of Port. This number changes for each producer every year based on the aggregate global demand for Port, weather conditions, grading of individual vineyards etc. If you're a producer, you get your Beneficio doled out to you every year and that's how much Port you can make. Regardless of how many grapes you have.

As you can imagine, this creates all kinds of interesting market incentives. Producers buying other producers' allocation rights, gaming the system, tweaking their wine grades. I think it is a bad thing, because it creates incentives to do things like letting vines that should be replaced stay in the ground, because you get more points for old vines.

Since the IVDP elders (the ruling body) don't read DAKT on the regular, this system is likely to stay in place for the time being. Or at least until I am appointed Global Wine Czar.

How this generally played out was that the producers would sort their grapes every year, and use the very best grapes for making whatever their Port allocation was, and then make a bunch of crappy still wines from whatever was left. The focus wasn't on the still wines; these would be sold in local cafes on the cheap, while the higher value Port went to the export market.

Now, about fifteen years ago, savvy producers starting thinking about the value in still wines (I think maybe because they wanted to go around the Beneficio process). Some of these stopped playing the allocation game and started using some of their really best grapes to make still wines. And some of these were downright amazing.

Enter the World's Leading Wine Influencer. I drank the shit out of these wines back in the day. You could routinely find big complex reds for $10 or even less. I mean, c'mon! Ten bucks?

Then came 2014, and fucking Wine Spectator.

That year, a handful of Portuguese wines made the WS Top 100 Wines list. Moreover, three of the top four wines on the list were from Portugal. The number one wine was a Port, but numbers three and four were still wines.

Everyone was all "WTF just happened?" Pretty embarrassing for all the hundred-point cabs to get soundly thrashed by a couple of cheap Portuguese wines, but confirms what I have always said - wine does not need to be expensive to be great.

Then, WS followed that up with a story saying that Portugal was the most exciting wine region on the planet. Prices doubled and tripled overnight. I'm still pissed about that.

That said, the economics did convince more of the Portuguese producers to get into the still wine thing, and today more and more great stuff is coming out of there every day. Silver linings...

Why Portuguese Still Wines are Dope AF:

These are big, complex reds with firm tannins, spice and earth notes, and a range of black and red fruit flavors. Now, it should be noted that in Portugal they have about thirty grape varieties that they make still wine from. You haven't heard of any of these. They have names like Tinta Roriz, Bastardo, Castelao, Tinta Cao, and Touriga Franca. Most of the still wines are a blend of some of these.

The Dr. Frank-N-Furter star of the show though is Touriga Nacional. Some winemakers are doing a straight up single variety Touriga Nacional, while other winemakers are using Touriga Nacional as the dominant base, but are carefully blending in other grapes to get a very specific flavor profile.

These wines are sometimes labeled as Touriga Nacional, sometimes as proprietary blends, and sometimes they will list the blends on the label. In any case, I am always looking for wines that are all or mostly Touriga Nacional. These generally come from the Douro region, so may be simply labeled Douro (for blends), or sometimes Douro Touriga Nacional.

Despite the run up in prices over the last few years, you can still get world class Touriga Nacional for decent values. Certain wines have unfortunately achieved cult status, like Chryseia, which continues to inch up in price. I think the current release is probably around $70. Not inexpensive, but will kick the shit out of a similarly priced Alexander Valley Silver Oak.

Now, our recommendations.

This first one is gonna be big and a bit oaky. You Napa lovers are gonna dig this bad boy.

Quinta do Vallado Touriga Nacional

This next one is a blend, and is less about being big, and more about being complex. It's also half the price. This is my jam.

Quinto do Crasto Superior

Drink Well!

DRINKING & KNOWING THINGS
#30: CORNAS

There are a handful of grapes that generally need no introduction. We typically refer to these as "international varieties" because they are grown all over the world. You know these – they are grapes like Cabernet Sauvignon, Chardonnay, Merlot etc.

And Syrah!

As the World's Leading Wine Influencer it falls upon my shoulders to determine whether or not a wine is Dope AF. This is a heavy responsibility, so I make sure I am up to the task by drinking a ton of wine. In the case of international varieties however, the onus is different. We've already determined that international varieties are Dope. The market has spoken. In this case, what is far more important is where in the world the best expressions of a particular international grape are. With a little bit of price to value analysis layered in.

Now, Syrah kicks ass. Whenever I am in the mood for a big ass red wine, Syrah is always in the decision matrix as a possibility. It has to be, because as previously mentioned, it kicks ass. The real challenge with Syrah is where to get it. They grow Syrah (or Shiraz if you are in Australia, mate) pretty much all over the world, in different styles and at price points ranging from $3 a bottle to $2000+ a bottle. I bet if you go into your local grocery store and find the wine aisle there will be a section dedicated purely to Syrah.

This makes it tough to figure out what is worth drinking. Like Snoop, imma break it down...

Why Syrah is Dope AF:
When done right, Syrah has big spice notes, primarily black pepper,

combined with some meaty almost bacon type flavors and aromas. The acid is strong without overwhelming, and the tannins are firm and moderate grained. It's a great accompaniment to any type of red meat, game, and especially bacon.

Side Note: Anything that pairs well with bacon is automatically Dope AF. On that note, wait for my upcoming Alsatian Pinot Gris DAKT...

+1 Side Note: There used to be a company called the Grateful Palate which did a bacon and Syrah of the month club, where they would ship you a package of artisanal bacon and Syrah every month. They don't do that anymore, more's the pity.

But I digress...

Back to Syrah – where to get it? In my opinion, the truest expression of Syrah comes from the birthplace of it – the Rhône Valley. There are definitely some real standouts from South Africa, Australia, and the US, but many of those wines are generally going to be heavily extracted and oaked. If like me you aren't a huge fan of that style it's best to stay focused on the Rhône. That's gonna be complicated enough.

Since the Rhône Valley is in France, these wines are going to be labeled by the town that they are from. The main ones are Hermitage, Crozes-Hermitage, St. Joseph and Cornas.

- Hermitage is generally very high quality, powerful, and elegant wines with prices to match.
- Crozes-Hermitage is not as refined as Hermitage, at a lower price point, and a bit more rustic.
- St. Joseph is like a mini Hermitage – similar style but not quite as complex.

Any of these three are going to be a good bet if you are looking for a kick ass Syrah.

But I am always on the lookout for Cornas.

Why Cornas is Dope AF:
First off, it's a little bit different terroir. All the other regions in the

northern Rhône lie along the river and get smashed every year with these super cold winds called Le Mistral that sweep down the river. This makes the grapes heat up and cool down every day and drives the complexity of all of the wines from that region.

Cornas though is a small little amphitheater-shaped valley, only about two hundred twenty acres in total, that is set back from the river and doesn't get hit with Le Mistral quite as much. So the grapes ripen differently

Cornas also has a special red-brown soil that is a bit unique. The name Cornas comes from the Celtic word for scorched earth.

What you end up with are these wines that are powerful as hell, and very rustic. I once called Cornas in an MW tasting session (I was right btw), and the instructor asked me what my tells were for Cornas. I gave this reply, which is very unscientific but I stand by it today. I replied, "For me Cornas is obviously Rhône Syrah, but it has a feral quality to it. It tastes like the kind of wine that Bacchus would pour at some riotous orgy in the forest."

As unscientific as that explanation was, a bunch of people nodded their heads and were like "Yeah I totally get that."

Historically I have had a Cornas aging rule similar to Barolo. I don't want to drink it unless it is a minimum of seven years old. That said, like in Barolo there are some producers now who are making a more modern style of Cornas that is approachable at a younger age.

Unlike Barolo though, I have an opinion on this debate. I think the rusticity and feral quality of Cornas is what makes it interesting and unique. The more modern styles are similar to what you might get in Crozes-Hermitage or St. Joseph. I don't want that! I want the Bacchus forest orgy party wine! If I want St. Joseph I will just buy St. Joseph....

Alas, though, the wheel of progress must churn forward, collateral damage to my forest party wine notwithstanding.

Anyway, since Cornas is so tiny the output is small. In total probably only about 45,000 cases are produced annually for the entire world. This is less than half of the annual production of Kendall Jackson Merlot. So you aren't going to see it everywhere, but it also isn't terribly difficult to find. Keep an eye out and when you see it, stock up. Expect prices for decent options to be in the $45-75 range.

Here's a couple of options:

The first is from one of the guys who is doing a more modern style. This is one of his flagship wines, priced accordingly. Caveat – I find an unacceptable level of faults in Colombo's wines, probably one bottle in six in my experience is faulted. Which is a sucky bet when you are laying down a hundred smacks. But still cheaper than a similar quality level Hermitage.

Jean Luc Colombo Les Ruchets Cornas

This other guy's stuff is fucking great at half the price.

Alain Voge Les Chaillees Cornas

Drink Well!!

Drinking & Knowing Things
#31: TIMORASSO

The world is full of thousands of local indigenous wine grapes. Some of these, like America's own Norton grape, are horrific, good solely for making a nasty bitter wine suitable as a home crafted insecticide and also probably causing blindness and dementia. Others, like Assyrtiko, are amazing and delicious. This massive proliferation of different grapes is mainly why in Europe they label the wines by what town they are made in. Because back in the day we didn't know what the different grapes were – we just knew that wine made in different towns tasted different.

Indigenous varietals are like Eminem songs. Some of them are absolutely spectacular. Others are boring and/or hard to swallow or take seriously. But when you find the spectacular ones they are usually super inexpensive, and also interesting. And a great conversation piece at parties. It just takes a lot of wading through a sea of uninteresting and sometimes crappy wines to find the gems. Also, sometimes it isn't the grape itself that is bad, but the winemaker fucked it up. So you generally have to try a few different examples of a wine before forming an opinion.

I'm inherently curious about wines, so I am always all in on trying something new. For a while I had this whole thing about going to wine stores and only buying wines that I had no idea what they were. Now that I know everything that game isn't as fun anymore.

Today I'm going to tell you all a pithy little tale about Timorasso.

Why Timorasso is Dope AF:
It's sometimes called the Italian Riesling.

Nuff said. All in.

Timorasso is another one of those grapes that almost went extinct but one ultra-passionate and moderately insane winemaker named Walter Massa refused to let it go and started planting a bunch of it in the early 1990s.

I had never even heard of this grape until a few years ago. One of the members in my weekly MW study group was this crazy Italian dude who owned a winery in Piedmont. I assumed he grew Nebbiolo. One day I asked him some sort of super esoteric question about Nebbiolo and he was like "No dude, I grow Timorasso."

I provided the appropriate response which was "WTF is Timorasso? Never heard of it."

His response: "Really? It's the Riesling of Italy."

Seeing as how I fucking love Riesling, I immediately began searching for Timorasso. I couldn't find it anywhere in the US. Spent a few months aggressively looking and then pretty much gave up. Every time I went into any wine shop I would ask them if they had Timorasso. No one, even the uber geeky wine shop folks (you know the type), had ever even heard of it.

Fast forward a couple of years. I found myself driving through Asheville, North Carolina. I stop for lunch and there's a little Podunk wine store with a sign out front saying "European Wines". Of course I wander in because why not. Dude comes up and asks if he can help me. I give the automatic "Yo, you guys got any Timorasso?" response. Dude nonchalantly replies with "yeah, it's over there" and waves his hand towards the back.

Holy fuck!

I was like no way does this crappy little wine store in the middle of BFE have Timorasso. I assumed the guy didn't know what he was talking about and was trying to pawn something else off on me not knowing he was dealing with the World's Leading Wine Influencer. Sure as shit though, they had some.

Side Note: Turns out the wine store owner was super into wine and I spent like an hour chatting with him about all kinds of weird shit. To the point where Ann began actively tugging at my shirt and whining like a petulant two-year-old trying to get me to leave.

I'll miss her.

We grab a couple of bottles and head off to the hotel. Chill them up in the mini-fridge and pop one open. It's as fantastic as promised. Does have a Riesling quality to it, but with a little more phenolic bitterness on the finish and great aromatics. A very interesting wine, which I would have loved to have tried with food. I think it would go amazing with spicy food, like yellow curry.

Since then I have continued to keep my eyes open for it, and have encountered it a few more times. The last time I saw it I bought a case, because I knew by then that it was tough to come by.

Now I know I bitched and complained about how the media can blow up certain wines, e.g. Portuguese still wines. In this case, I think we could do with a little blowing up of Timorasso. I think this wine has real potential and we are only scratching the surface.

Wine Spectator – take note!

Here's today's recommendation. It's from Vietti, which if you recall from the Arneis DAKT is the winery in Piedmont that is paying attention to some of the indigenous varietals. You can give this a try if you want to jump on the Timorasso bandwagon with me.

Pro Tip: 2018 is Vietti's first ever Timorasso vintage. Which alone makes it interesting.

Side Note: Vietti actually buys some of their Timorasso grapes from my crazy Italian buddy.

Vietti Timorasso

That said, the long con here is that I am trying to get you all to play the "Yo, you got any Timorasso?" game when you all visit your local wine shops. That way, those folks will ask the distributors, who will ask the importers and if we do it right eventually we will get more options available here in the states, and we can all overindulge on Timorasso and smile. As members of the DAKT Street Team I expect you all to do your part...even those of you from Texas.

As always, Drink Well!!

DRINKING & KNOWING THINGS
#32: VIN JAUNE

Some of you are going to hate this wine.

Which is fine. I didn't love this wine the first time I tried it. It's unique. There's nothing else like it in the wine world. Since it's different, the first time you try it you will be like WTF. Your taste buds will expect one thing but will get another, your brain will short circuit and you will be "oh hell no".

Kimchi – you may recall I made you try this in NYC. You were not happy.

But stick with it. I had to try it probably two or three times before I began to love it, and now it is one of my go-to wines for food pairings as well as one of my all-time favorites. It's also one of those wines that if you order it at a restaurant multiple people are likely to come out from the back and come talk to you because you are a) interesting and b) know your wine.

There's massive street cred in ordering a wine at a large dinner and then have someone come out and kiss your ass in front of everyone for being a wine expert.

Side Note: I was with some of the DAKT Street Team in Alsace a few years back and I introduced them to the nutty deliciousness that is Vin Jaune and they all loved it straight from jump. We drank the hell out of Vin Jaune that entire trip. So you may like it right away. But probably not.

+1 Side Note: Feel free to steal "nutty deliciousness" as a wine tasting note. You're welcome.

Why Vin Jaune is Dope AF:

First off it's from the Jura region in France. Everything from the Jura is Dope AF. So there's that. More importantly it is this great alliance of refreshing acidity, a full body with lifted aromatics, and a lot of nutty deliciousness. It is crazy good with food and also great on its own.

Why Vin Jaune is Unique AF:

Technically Vin Jaune is more of a wine style than a wine. But they are almost always labeled Vin Jaune so this is what you would look for.

Here's why it's special. The producers start with the Savagnin grape. Nope, that is not a misspelling. It has zero relation to Cabernet Sauvignon or Sauvignon Blanc. It just sounds similar. This is a white grape that on its own is boring and neutral. The winemaker goes through the regular process of making a normal still wine, which ends up being boring and neutral.

> **Pro Tip:** Some of the folks in the Jura are experimenting with Chardonnay right now as well. We're starting to see a bit more of that. Not sure I am supportive of this. I may have to put my foot down.

After the wine is made is where shit gets real. They put the wine into neutral oak barrels and they don't top the barrels up, leaving a bit of an air gap at the top. Then they leave it alone.

As the wine ages for the first couple of years, it begins to evaporate and also oxidize, because the whole surface area at the top of the barrel is exposed to air. Over time, a film of yeast forms over the top of the wine. Eventually, the whole top of the wine is covered with a blanket of yeast.

Once the blanket is fully formed (which takes a couple of years) the wine is now protected from oxygen. It no longer oxidizes. Instead, the flavors from the yeast begin to permeate the wine. Much like the way that in Champagne flavors emerge from aging the wine on the dead yeast cells inside the bottle over a few years, giving Vin Jaune the same nutty, toasty brioche flavors that we enjoy in kickass Vintage and Grand Cru Champagnes.

After six years in the barrel, where the first part is oxidative aging and the second part is aging under a blanket of yeast, the wine is ready. Probably the best way to describe the final product is that it tastes like a Vintage Champagne might if it wasn't bubbly.

Pro Tip: Sometimes they don't wait the full six years, and pull the wine out early. Then it is called Vin Ouille instead. It has some of the yeast flavors, but much more subdued. If I am drinking it on its own without food I often prefer Vin Ouille to Vin Jaune.

+1 Pro Tip: They bottle Vin Jaune in these kind of funky shaped tapered and/or short bottles that are only 620ml instead of the standard 750ml. This is because they basically say you are buying the original wine at regular scale, but a bunch of it has evaporated over the six years so you only get 620ml of the finished wine. Not sure that entirely makes sense, but somehow these guys have gotten away with it for many years.

+2 Pro Tip: These special bottles are called "clavelins".

+3 Pro Tip: The part of the wine that evaporates is sometimes called the Angel's Share. Cause, ya know, the Angels come down from heaven and help themselves to nutty deliciousness while we are sleeping. Oh those crazy Angels...

Bottom Line: Vin Jaune has a strange name, comes in a weird size, in a funky bottle, from an unknown grape, and tastes super different than any other wine. What's not to love about that? This is gonna get attention at your next soiree for sure. In part because a bunch of people will hate it. Fuck them. It's rad.

Side Note: As the World's Leading Wine Influencer I may need to establish a new ratings tier – Rad AF.

Now, our recommendations. As mentioned, most of the time the wine will be labeled Vin Jaune. Except if it is from a special AOC (physical area) called Château-Chalon. Then the wines will be labeled Château-Chalon and probably won't say Vin Jaune on the label, because you are supposed to know already.

Side Note: Back in the early 20th century the pre-eminent wine writer in Paris was this dude who operated under the pen name Curnonsky. He counted Château-Chalon among the five great French white wines, alongside Montrachet, Château d'Yquem, Coulée de Serrant and Château Grillet. Some good company there...

Vin Jaune isn't the easiest to find, and Château-Chalon even more difficult. When you find some, stock up because these wines will age for a very long time. Get two at least because you are probably not gonna like the first bottle.

Here's a Château-Chalon :

Domaine Jean Macle Château-Chalon

And a regular old Vin Jaune:

Jacques Puffeney Vin Jaune

Pro Tip: Try this with any soft cheese and prepare to lose your damn mind.

As always, Drink Well!

Drinking & Knowing Things
#33: JURANÇON

I bet that all of us can look back on pretty much any period of our lives and laugh at the dumb, naïve people we were at that time, and what we thought was "cool". Please refer to the entire decade of the 1980s for more information on this.

When I first started getting into wine about twenty-five years ago, I was aware of both kinds of wine – red and white. But I only wanted red. And the biggest, most powerful reds I could find. White wine was only for sissies and people who listen to Jason Mraz. But I repeat myself...

Anyway, as I went along my wine journey I began to get exposed to more and more options, and now I bet I drink more white wine than reds. I also began to realize that my binary red/white classification system was faulty. There are actually shitloads of different wines available and for me to say I was a "red wine guy" or a "white wine guy" was extremely limiting. Consequently, I began exploring all kinds of different options.

Side Note: I can't wait until twenty-five years from now and I look back at what an idiot I am today! I wonder what I'll be drinking then...

Anyway, one of the types of wines I encountered along the way was the proverbial sweet wine. And I'm not talking about a white Zinfandel with fifteen grams of residual sugar. I'm talking about thick syrupy wines with several hundred grams of residual sugar, that scream Type 2 diabetes the second you open them.

The first one of these I ever tried was a Sauternes. I was like what in the holy hell is this? This is worse than the foul concoction served in the South that they somehow think is iced tea. Spoiler: it isn't. Drinking this every day is why half of you need scooters to navigate Walmart.

But then I tried Sauternes with Fois Gras. Mind blown.

Side Note: I once attended a dinner at Château Rieussec where they had a traditional wine pairing with every dish and an optional Sauternes pairing with every dish. Mind blown again!

This continues to reinforce my point that all wines have some sort of purpose and it's up to us to figure out what that is for us.

Since I am what some judgey haters might term as "obsessive/compulsive" about wine, I of course leaned way in on sweet wines. And found that they are also awesome. In their own way.

Today we are gonna talk about one of my favorites – **Jurançon!**

Why Jurançon is Dope AF:

Jurançon is a small region in the south of France near the Spanish border (not quite within thirty miles, Daniel you geography fascist, but close). This area should not be confused with the Jura region (which produces awesome reds and nutty delicious whites). That's a different place in France with a similar name. Just to make it even more confusing, there actually is a grape in southern France called Jurancon (without the little dingleberry under the C), which is not used in the region of Jurançon, nor in the Jura. Welcome to France...

In Jurançon, they grow white grapes you never heard of like Gros Manseng, Petit Manseng and Courbu. They use these grapes to make moderately interesting still wines, and some of the best sweet wines in the world.

Side Note: The winemakers' industry association in Jurançon at one point had a marketing campaign where the tag line was "Manseng means Jurançon means Sex".

+1 Side Note: The only non-standard varietal we have growing in Bhutan is Petit Manseng. Cause, ya know...sex. Well that and it is super rain tolerant. But I'm sticking with sex for the marketing materials.

These wines are brilliant. They aren't as syrupy sweet as a Sauternes or Tokaji. They basically pick the grapes later in the season, when they have shriveled up so the water to sugar ratio is higher and they have a little bit of noble rot some years. The winemaker decides when to pick, so you will see a range of sweetness levels depending on the winemaker's preference. But even the sweetest styles probably won't be quite as sweet and heavy as a Sauternes. They have amazing fresh acidity and tropical fruit aromas that somehow balance the sweetness perfectly.

Pro Tip: One of my MW buddies says his tell for Jurançon is a candied pineapple flavor. I think that's not a bad call.

The wines that are sweet will be labeled Jurançon, whereas the dry wines will be labeled Jurançon sec. "Sec" in wine means "mostly dry". For me, the Jurançon sec wines are ok. There's nothing offensive about them nor anything super interesting. They are easy sipping patio wines and they're typically pretty cheap, usually under $20. Worth trying but not worth getting all spun up about.

The sweet wines are what we want. As with a lot of the weird shit I am into, these wines are not the easiest to come across. Albertsons is not gonna have a Jurançon section. But you can find them with a bit of effort. And these are definitely wines that when you find them you should buy a six-pack at least. You're gonna want to break these out after dinner, maybe with a lemon tart or a key lime pie. And I promise that you will finish the bottle and spend some time deliberating about opening up another. It's that good.

Side Note: I once hosted a dinner at a conference with about ten or twelve people. I ordered a Jurançon with dessert, and we finished the bottle quickly. People demanded we get another so we did. Three more times. I still get asked about what that dessert wine was – not just by people that were there but by people who heard that we drank this amazing wine. Jurançon, baby!!! That's what's up...

I have a very strong producer preference here. There's a dude (deceased now) named Didier Dagueneau who was well known as the best winemaker in the Loire, where he primarily made these spectacular Sauvignon Blanc wines. These are generally thought of as some of the best Sauvignon Blanc in the world (hmmm, maybe I should do a DAKT on that...stay tuned). He decided he was going to get on the Manseng train, and started also making a Jurançon called Les Jardines des Babylone (the Gardens of Babylon). This is simply spectacular wine. This might be in my top twenty all-time list.

Side Note: That was what we were drinking in the four-bottle story above.

+1 Side Note: Dagueneau was a complete badass and also used to race motorcycle sidecars professionally. Which is Dope AF and also batshit crazy. If you want to kill three minutes watch this shit. https://www.youtube.com/watch?v=Bp28Dev-pOc

It's expensive but awesome. Buy this immediately.

Didier Dagueneau Les Jardin de Babylone Jurançon

If you aren't convinced to drop eighty smacks, feel free to limp in with a $20 half-bottle of this...

Domaine Cauhape Symphony de Novembre Jurançon

Drink Well!

DRINKING & KNOWING THINGS
#34: PASSE-TOUT-GRAINS

If you have been good little students, diligently studying the erudition and wisdom ensconced within DAKT, you are likely aware that I am a fan of Burgundy, specifically the red wine from the Pinot Noir grape.

And by "fan" I mean that I am fucking obsessed with it. Let's not forget I have a giant tattoo of the La Tache vineyard across my entire chest. Moreover, I have strong opinions about Burgundy. There are producers over there that IMHO are screwing things up. Prices are absurd. Labeling is beyond complex. The Grand Cru and Premier Cru systems are unknowably complicated.

But the wines are spectacular. And if you've been good little DAKT students, you also know about the not-so-secret secret of Burgundy which is the southern Beaujolais region and the Gamay grape. Some great wines come out of Beaujolais – they are just different than the Pinot Noir wines from the northern part of Burgundy.

So what have we learned?

Pinot Noir from Burgundy is fucking awesome.

Beaujolais (Gamay) from Burgundy can be fucking awesome.

How could we possibly make these even better?

Some of you have figured out where I am going with this.

We'll mix them together and create a Burgundy love child!!!!!

Yep. That's a thing. It's called Passe-Tout-Grains or sometimes Passetoutgrains. They'll be labeled Borgogne Passe-Tout-Grains. They have the pedigree and terroir of some of the best wine in the world, but are super cheap, comparatively. This is the real secret of Burgundy.

Why Passe-Tout-Grains is Dope AF:

Well, it sounds like Passed Out Grains if you say it the American way. And I am always up for drinking anything named Passed Out. You all know goddamn well if you showed up at a party with a bottle of something called Passed Out you would be the hero that night.

Apart from the cool name, the wine is great too. Pinot and Gamay are similar in structure, both light bodied, fruit driven, and potentially some spiciness or earth. So it isn't like when your kid creates a horrific cocktail at Burger King by mixing Mountain Dew and Dr. Pepper together out of the fountain. These grapes complement each other nicely without seeming disjointed and completely out of place. They mix the grapes together before they ferment, so the grapes will co-ferment together and extract the flavors during fermentation as a team as opposed to blending them together later.

Pro Tip: Passe-Tout-Grains means basically "throw it all in". Essentially this means that you can mix everything together.

+1 Pro Tip: Which means, even though the wines must be a minimum of 30% Pinot and 15% Gamay, that pretty much all other Burgundy grapes are fair game as well, like Chardonnay and Aligote (although the whites are limited to 15% of the total blends).

Side Note: I think the whole reason this became an allowable wine is that the farmers were mixing all of the leftover shit together after the harvest and someone was all "Hey this is pretty good, we oughta sell it." So they made an AOC around it.

+1 Side Note: The above Side Note is my opinion and not backed by any research and/or data. Too much effort...

That said, some of the best Pinot producers in Burgundy (e.g. D'angerville, Lafarge) make a Passe-Tout-Grains strictly because they love it. They could repurpose those vineyards for higher price point wine, but there's something about Passe-Tout-Grains that a handful of maniacal folks are basically saying fuck it, we like it, it's our heritage and we're gonna keep making it, and we don't care what you think. I love that attitude.

Now, these wines are never going to rival the Premier Crus of Burgundy. But they could be on par with the named Crus of Beaujolais. And they are going to be cheap. It's gonna be hard to pay more than $25 for a bottle of this. So if you want some great quality and flavors of Burgundy at a much lower price it's a super option. The wine will have bit of complexity, great acidity and fruit, and will be deliciously easy to drink. Plus no one knows about this wine in the US, not even many of the Burgundy-philes, so it is instant wine street cred. You start asking your somm for this and you'll blow his or her mind.

Pro Tip: Because the rules are so broad about what goes into these wines, you'll get a high degree of variation from rosé wines, to lighter fruitier reds, to more smoky complex reds. The World's Leading Wine Influencer rule of thumb here is only buy the ones that are strictly Pinot and Gamay. None of that white grape nonsense in our Passe-Tout-Grains...

On to our recommendation:

D'Angerville Passe-Tout-Grains

Note: I'm stoked to put a D'Angerville option in here. If you drink Burgundy, that name needs no introduction. If you don't drink Burgundy – immediately stop reading these DAKTs and don't come back until you start.

Those of you who did the New York Wine Marathon a couple of years back will remember D'Angerville's Volnay as the best wine of the day, which we drank at Corkbuzz right before that infamous shitshow photo.

However, if you want to go on a vision quest, you can add any Passe-Tout-Grains as a follow-up question at the wine store when the guy tells you they don't have any Timorasso. That's a strong play...

Drink Well!

DRINKING & KNOWING THINGS
#35: PINOT GRIGIO - PART 1

I know some of you read the title for this week and were like "What the hell, Mike? Pinot Grigio?"

But reserve judgment for the time being. You're about to get some science dropped on you.

First, we have already established that Pinot Noir is awesome. Over the years, mutations in the vineyard created three different kinds of Pinot: Pinot Noir, which is red. Pinot Blanc (or Bianco if you're Italian), which is white. And Pinot Gris (or Grigio), which is technically "gray" but makes a white wine.

Of the three, Pinot Grigio probably has the worst reputation. This is because it can make a very neutral wine at a low price point. This makes it almost the best possible by-the-glass option at US restaurants. It isn't offensive to anyone, because it is bland. People might hate Chardonnay or Sauvignon Blanc, but they will grudgingly drink a Pinot Grigio if there aren't other options. Moreover, it is a great gateway drug for people who are new to wine drinking. It's completely tolerable; the Wonder Bread of wine. Or maybe a better analogue is the Dave Matthews Band of wine. Bland, boring, and created to appeal to the lowest common denominator. But no one hates it. It will suffice.

Consequently, in the US we import ridiculous amounts of Pinot Grigio, and almost all of it is a weak insipid, inoffensive wine. It is, by volume, the most imported wine in the US by a significant margin.

We then chill it down to very cold levels before serving it, which represses aromas and flavors even more. You may have found yourselves in a restaurant and all they had by the glass was Pinot Grigio and the glass was literally condensed over when they handed it to you. It's like a glass of lemon-flavored cold water.

I do have to hand it to the Italians. They have cracked the code on how to sell Pinot Grigio to the Americans. I just find the wines boring as hell.

Mostly.

That said, we have already agreed that Pinot is awesome. So why is it that Pinot Grigio sucks?

The answer is – not all of it sucks. The issue is the good stuff is not wasted on exports to the US. I'm sure somewhere in northern Italy right now there's a winery where Mario and Luigi are quaffing glasses of amazing Pinot Grigio while preparing stuff for export and they are all laughing and stepping it down with water and saying shit like "It still has too much flavor and body – dump another fifty gallons of water into the tank – the dumb Americans will never know."

Side Note: While they are correct that we dumb Americans will never know - technically that is illegal. So that is a purely "hypothetical" scene above. That said, I don't understand how they can literally strip all the body, flavor and aroma out of a wine. Maybe it is just that they crank up the yield per vine to huge levels in order to maximize volume rather than character.

I suppose it is like eating a plate of macaroni and cheese at a bistro in Rome, vs. tossing an Easy Mac in the microwave. The kids love that Easy Mac but it bears no comparison to the rich delectable dishes available on pretty much every street corner in Italy.

Why Pinot Grigio is Dope AF:

Well, the boring insipid stuff has a place I suppose. If my two options at a restaurant were cold lemon water or Pinot Grigio, and it was one hundred degrees out and it was lunchtime, a glass of that could be refreshing, and I would consider opting for the Pinot Grigio over the lemon water. Because it has alcohol in it.

But what I really want is the purest expression of Pinot Grigio. When done in a more ambitious style, Pinot Grigio can be a rich, textured wine with a hint of copper color, lean minerality and a phenolic finish. Some of the producers are experimenting with oak aging – generally in more neutral barrels. The goal isn't to make an oaky Pinot Grigio, but use the oak aging to provide a fuller body, more texture, and sometimes a bit of oxidative aging.

These wines are anything but the boring lemon-water styles we typically see here in the US, and are generally going to blow people's minds because they aren't used to Pinot Grigio that is as rich and layered as these.

Side Note: when I say rich and layered I mean in comparison to the standard $8/bottle Pinot Grigio you see in grocery stores or by the glass at Buco di Beppo. They'll never be as full bodied as Grand Cru Burgundy, so don't expect that. On the other hand, they are going to be $20 instead of $800 and are delicious.

Where to Find Dope AF Pinot Grigio:

Northern Italy. Full Stop. That said, one needs to be a bit careful here because this is where the boring and insipid stuff comes from too.

Let's start with some simple rules. Italy has four quality classifications. We want wines that fall into one of the top two. These are called DOC or DOCG wines. (DOCG is better). You can tell because there will be a little black label over top of the bottle that will say DOC or DOCG. Look for that.

Now – that in and of itself is a good start, but not the full answer. The next thing we want is to focus on which DOCs or DOCGs are making the highest quality. And there are a ton of small ones. It is impossible to memorize all the little specifics of all the hundreds of DOCs and DOCGs. Don't bother trying.

But as the World's Leading Wine Influencer, I am going to try to make it easier for you with a simple rule. Look for bottles that are labeled either Collio or Colli Orientale. If you want a mnemonic, I use an image of Lassie lapping up a dish full of Pinot Grigio. Cause you know, she's a Collie. Also it's fun to see what happens next when good girl Lassie gets turnt da fuck up on Pinot Grigio.

A small warning though. Both of these DOCGs produce white wines from other grapes as well. We want one that specifically states Pinot Grigio on the label. Otherwise it is likely a blend, or perhaps another grape altogether like Fruili or Malvasia.

Now our recommendations:

Here's one from Collio Gorziano. (A sub-zone of Collio. You don't need to remember this – just look for the Collio.)

Mario Schiopetto Pinot Grigio Collio

And here's one from Colli Orientale. Terlato is a solid producer.

Terlato Pinot Grigo Colli Orientale

And stay tuned for next week's Pinot Grigio – Part Two.

Drink Well! (I never would have thought I would attach Drink Well to a glass of Pinot Grigio, but here we are....)

DRINKING & KNOWING THINGS
#36: PINOT GRIGIO - PART 2

Usually when I use one of my advanced foreshadowing techniques I tease you with a wine for a while before delivering the goods. Like when you go see a Tool show and they play weird music and trippy videos for like thirty minutes until the crowd is whipped into a frothy screaming mess and finally the lights drop and the show starts and people go crazy.

In my mind this is how I see all of you each week, staring at your inbox and hitting refresh every sixty seconds, anxiously awaiting your weekly dosage of DAKT and then when it finally drops you start screaming and cheering.

Side Note: feel free to film yourself waiting and post those videos on Instagram and tag @drinkingandknowing.

You are in luck this week. Because I am going to talk about Pinot Gris, along with the bacon pairing I teased you with a couple of weeks ago.

Now, Pinot Gris is the exact same grape as Pinot Grigio. It's just that the Italians call it Pinot Grigio and the rest of the world calls it Pinot Gris.

Pro Tip: Except in Germany and Austria where they call it Grauburgunder. Because Pinot Gris doesn't have enough consonants, and is pronounceable, which is a violation of German wine law.

Why Pinot Gris is Dope AF:

While this wine is made in many different countries around the world, the style tends to be pretty similar. In contrast to Pinot Grigio, Pinot Gris is going to be a richer, more textured wine. These wines are going to be lower in acid than their Italian counterparts, and will generally have higher alcohol (bonus!) and a broader array of fruit aromas and flavors, often in the tropical fruit area like mango and cantaloupe.

Moreover, they will often have a slight amount of residual sugar, and occasionally be made in a sweeter off-dry style. It's a great food wine and also great as a stand alone wine.

Where to Get Dope Pinot Gris:

Oregon and New Zealand are starting to produce some Pinot Gris that as the World's Leading Wine Influencer I pronounce "acceptable". However, my only go-to for Pinot Gris is Alsace, France.

A brief word on Alsace. This is a tiny little strip of land, maybe forty miles long and six or so miles wide. It's on the other side of the Vosges Mountains nestled between Germany and France. This area has changed ownership between countries so many times over the centuries that the people there have ceased to give a fuck about either Germany or France and do their own thing. And their own thing is make the best food and wine possible and then drink the wine and eat the food.

Not a bad way of living.

Side Note: I have heard that Alsace has more Michelin starred restaurants than any other place in France. Which is saying a lot, but I believe it. One time I was there we stayed in a small hotel that had like nine rooms and the café in the hotel lobby had two Michelin stars. The food there is that spectacular. If you want to do the greatest food and wine trip as inexpensively as possible nowhere on Earth beats Alsace. It also is one of the most beautiful wine regions in the world and the people are so friendly you forget you are in France.

Alsace produces a boatload of wine, and much of it is good quality yet inexpensive. I think that dollar for dollar Alsace represents some of the best wine values in the world. You can buy great Alsatian wine all day long for $15-20.

That said, while I enjoy the values there, they produce some extremely high-quality wines that are simply not to be missed.

The plucky Alsatians have their own wine system. Which I think is due in part to the back and forth ownership over the years and due in part to their capacity to say fuck it we are gonna do our own thing. In a marked departure from both French and German wine regulatory tradition, they have opted for a simplistic structure. There's Grand Cru wine and then non-Grand Cru wine.

> **Pro Tip:** It's actually slightly more complicated than that, but that's all you really need to know. And still waaaaayyyyyyyy easier than Germany or Burgundy.

Alsace is dotted with a ton of small medieval villages, all of which make wine. Generally speaking, they find the best vineyard in a specific village and they designate that vineyard as Grand Cru. Most villages have a Grand Cru, but not all of them. Overall there are fifty-one vineyards that are designated as Grand Cru, and the wines will be labeled with the name of the producer, the name of the vineyard, the words "Grand Cru", and then the variety. Example: Domaine Schlumberger Spiegel Grand Cru Pinot Gris.

The presence of a bunch of long Germanic words on the label can throw you off. But don't stress – all you want to do is look for the distinctive Alsatian bottle which is a long skinny phallus (called a flute), and then look for the words Grand Cru. If you stick with that you'll be ok.

> **Pro Tip:** There are four grapes allowed in Grand Cru vineyards. Pinot Gris, Riesling, Gewurztraminer and Muscat. This trick works with all four.

> **+1 Pro Tip:** There's a ton of terroir variation across the fifty-one Grand Crus, so expect that the wine will vary. A super cool thing to do is to grab wines made from the same grape (e.g. Riesling) from two different Grand Crus and drink them against each other and note how different they are.

> **+2 Pro Tip:** There's a ton of winemaker style differences as well. Don't try your first bottle ever and then jump to any conclusions. You are gonna love some and probably not so much on others. Try

a few. But it's pretty easy to find Alsatian Grand Cru wines for $20-30, so it won't break the bank.

On to our recommendations:

Here's the aforementioned one from Schlumberger.

Domaine Schlumberger Spiegel Grand Cru Pinot Gris

Then there are a handful of Alsatian producers that make world class wine at a higher price point. Here's one from Boxler.

Albert Boxler Sommerberg Grand Cru Pinot Gris

And a ridiculous one from Zind-Humbrecht, which IMHO is one of the top producers in Alsace.

Zind Humbrecht Rangen Grand Cru Pinot Gris

Side Note: Olivier Humbrecht is an MW. Just saying...

+1 Side Note: The Rangen vineyard is one of the steepest vineyards I have ever been in. It is like a fucking cliff. I have no idea how they farm it. And Mina almost killed all of us by trying to turn around the rental car on the tiny little access road. I still have nightmares...

Finally, for one of my all-time favorite food and wine pairings – go down to the butcher and get some high-quality bacon. Fry this up with a little bit of brown sugar and maple syrup. Chill up a bottle of Alsatian Pinot Gris and eat a plate of bacon while drinking the Pinot Gris. Feel free to collapse into orgiastic convulsions if needed. You're welcome...

Drink Well!

Drinking & Knowing Things
#37: ASSYRTIKO

I figured because we went mainstream with Pinot Grigio the last couple of weeks that it was necessary to jump back into obscure grape territory – in this case straight to Greece! (You're welcome, Jim...)

Greece is chock full of indigenous varieties with crazy unpronounceable names. While I have been there, and toured wine regions and drank a bunch of different wines, I would not even begin to represent myself as an authority on Greek wine, even as an MW candidate. It's an extremely unique and complicated wine country. Which alone makes it cool.

I will also say that I have had a fair bit of Greek wine that doesn't come anywhere near the neighborhood of our Dope AF threshold. So don't go crazy with the whole "Greek wines are awesome" narrative. But some are.

Side Note: Mr. Humphries has submitted a formal request through proper channels for me to include more metal references in DAKT as apparently this has been a relatively large shortcoming in both Wine Spectator and Wine Enthusiast wine write-ups. Which is understandable. Not everyone can be the World's Leading Wine Influencer.

Consequently, feel free to think about Greece as the Slipknot of wine. A lot of it can be harsh, guttural, with more pageantry than is truly necessary. Overall not horrible, but not that enjoyable either. But occasionally there's a flash of genius that makes you think, hmmmm, maybe I need to be spending a bit more time with this.

Furthering that analogy, let me introduce you to the "Wait and Bleed" of Greek wine – Assyrtiko!

Why Assyrtiko is Dope AF:

It's the only known European grape vine that is resistant to Phylloxera and blight. So that's pretty cool. This also means that they don't need to graft American roots onto the vines to make them survive, like they have to do everywhere else in Europe. Which means when you drink Assyrtiko you are drinking it exactly the way it has been grown for thousands of years. History in a glass.

Also, most of the vines are super old. In certain areas you can find Assyrtiko vines that are over three hundred years old. So if you buy into the argument that old vines are better than you should be all about the Assyrtiko. I would bet that on average Assyrtiko vines are older than any other varietal in the world.

> **Pro Tip:** I'm not sure I agree with the whole "old vines are better" argument but it makes for good marketing copy for lots of wineries. Maybe I need to do a DAKT on that...#foreshadowing.

Assyrtiko is a white wine that is all about texture and structure as opposed to fruit flavors. It's a lean wine with smoky undertones and ripping high acidity. Moreover it usually has reasonably high alcohol (bonus!) which makes it a bit unique in that generally alcohol and acid are trade-offs – if one is high than the other one tends to be medium at best. Not so much with Assyrtiko. The Greeks get it done...

Where to Get Assyrtiko:

Assyrtiko originated on the island of Santorini, and that is where the best stuff comes from. They grow it all over the country now, but the best examples still are from Santorini. The combination of scorching hot island sun gets the grapes super ripe, but the cooling ocean winds keep the acidity high. Also, Santorini is a volcano, so the grapes grow in this volcanic ash that contributes to the smoky minerality. Wines from Santorini will also have the word "Santorini" on the label so look for that. Avoid the stuff from Naoussa. It's meh.

> **Pro Tip:** On Santorini, the winds blow so damn hard that they have to weave the vines on the ground into a basket thing that looks like a bird's nest and the grapes grow on the inside of the nest

like tiny little bird's eggs. Seriously. Take a second and Google Santorini grape vine images. They are trippy as hell.

+1 Pro Tip: If you want to get super nerdy about it, that bird's nest thing is called a koulara.

Side Note: Another super cool thing that some of the wineries on Santorini do is age their wines in the ocean. They seal the wines with a special synthetic cork that is completely watertight, and then they fill up these giant lobster cage things with wine bottles and toss the whole thing into the ocean for a few years. The water provides a constant cool temperature, the wine is kept away from the harmful rays of the sun, and the environment is completely free from oxygen (yes, Dr. Eklund, I am aware that there is oxygen in water but wine bottles don't have gills, so they are safe...). The point is that under water is a pretty kickass place to age wine gracefully.

Lastly, I would be remiss if I didn't mention that some wineries also make a sweet style of Assyrtiko, by drying out the grapes into raisins and then pressing the raisins. These can be delicious as well, but are screamingly different than the lean racy mineral driven style that is more typical. Keep an eye out when buying Assyrtiko to make sure you are getting the style you want. Usually the sweet ones will be labeled "vinsanto".

I should point out that Assyrtiko is not that difficult to find. It's the kind of thing you would typically find at not just wine stores but also hipster places like Whole Foods or Trader Joe's. But if you want a recommendation here's an iconic one and a great example of how it's done on Santorini.

Gaia Assyrtiko

As always, Drink Well!

DRINKING & KNOWING THINGS
#38: SAUVIGNON BLANC, PART 1

My apologies for not sending out a DAKT last week. I know it clearly created issues and anxiety for people because I was inundated with thousands of emails and videos of people weeping inconsolably and apparently there were also some riots in weird cities like Portland. It's quite possible that the rioting may have been unrelated to last week's missing DAKT but it's not entirely clear what the riots were about so I'll count it as a DAKT issue. I'll refrain from commenting on the unmarked vans but let's just say that those of you who persist on drinking young Napa Cabs sometimes get sent away for "reconditioning". We know who you are...

But rightfully so the discontent. What on earth are you folks going to drink over the weekend without the World's Leading Wine Influencer as your spirit guide? That's right...probably Bourbon and Diet Mountain Dew or something terrible like that.

In all seriousness I had some medical shit done and was under the influence of heavy narcotics last week. I tried briefly to draft something but it came out like "wine good....drink more wine...me like...drinky drinky..." Since that sort of information is only useful to Erik, I elected to skip a week and pick up again this week. Sorry to everyone whose weekend was completely ruined.

For this week we are gonna lean in a bit on another well-known grape – Sauvignon Blanc. This is another one of those grapes that they grow everywhere in the world and make in various styles. I think in many cases Sauvignon Blanc has a well-deserved reputation of making a decent wine at an approachable price point. Much of it is unremarkable. But there are some standouts. Let's discuss, class...

Why Sauvignon Blanc is Dope AF:

I'm gonna call it SB throughout our discussion, because it is a pain in the ass to continually type Sauvignon Blanc. SB is a very versatile grape, and as mentioned, is made in a variety of different styles. For example, many people don't know that the deliciously sweet wines of Sauternes are mostly SB. But let's set the sweet styles aside for the time being and focus on the dry styles.

As a dry wine, SB is typically described as crisp or refreshing. It generally has high angular acid, and a range of fruit flavors from tropical to citrus depending on the climate where it is grown. Hotter climates generally will tend more to the tropical side and cooler climates will lean more towards citrus. In almost all cases, SB will also have a green character to it. I've heard this described as "grassy" or "green bell pepper" or even "canned asparagus".

Pro Tip: Technically the term for this green aroma/taste is "pyrazines". If you want to sound super knowledgeable about wine feel free to drop that bad boy e.g. "Wow this SB has a ton of pyrazines."

+1 Pro Tip: Technically the scientific term is "methoxypyrazine" so if some Cornell professor or asshole is trying to be cool by throwing around "pyrazines" feel free to raise the stakes on them e.g "Yes, I agree, there is a plethora of methoxypyrazine on this wine."

Side Note: This green character makes it quite easy to identify SB in a blind tasting. If you smell anything green, SB is a solid call. I once watched a teenage Baby Mike completely destroy a sommelier in Chicago by smelling a Marlborough SB and calling it Marlborough SB without tasting it. The dude started jumping up and down screaming "This kid called the wine correctly just on the nose".

+1 Side Note: Marlborough SB happened to be the only wine that Baby Mike knew so he just got crazy lucky that it was the first wine poured.

+2 Side Note: To his credit, Baby Mike refused to smell any of the later wines with a "Nah, I already nailed your simple game" flick of his wrist. So he went out on top. Well played, sir...

I drink three types of SB, for different reasons. We're gonna talk about one of them today and then pick up the other two next week.

The first main type of SB I drink is from the Loire Valley. Yep, the same Loire Valley that makes the world's best Chenin Blanc and the world's best Cab Franc. This region is the fucking bomb.

Now, you are all knowledgeable about how wine labels in France work – i.e. they are labeled by the name of the town the wine is made in. So there's no need for me to mention it again, except for Erik. The two towns (AOCs) in the Loire that make the best SB are Sancerre and Pouilly-Fumé, and the wines will be labeled as such.

Pro Tip: Most SB made in the US is labeled SB. Mondavi however labels its SB as "Fume Blanc" which derives from Pouilly-Fumé (that which of course would have a tougher sell in the US than the kindler, gentler Fume Blanc designation).

Sancerre and Pouilly-Fumé are similar in the sense that the climate is pretty similar between the two regions. They literally are on opposite sides of the river from each other in a cooler northernly location. This means that they will both have high lean acidity, and will be more on the citrus side of the fruit spectrum. I often get grapefruit on both of them.

But there are some subtle differences. For me, Pouilly-Fumé tends to be more dense and fruit-driven than its Sancerre cousin. Sancerre for me often has higher minerality and is more precise. Maybe a good analogue here is the Hilton sisters. Paris is the more expressive rounder Pouilly-Fumé whereas Nicky is the more austere and focused Sancerre.

Which is better? Well, depends on your tastes. I prefer Sancerre over Pouilly-Fumé almost always. However, Pouilly-Fumé tends to be cheaper on average than Sancerre, so if you were to factor in the wine enjoyment per dollar ratio it is quite possible that Pouilly-Fumé would come out on top.

That said, there are some producers on the Sancerre side who are really trying to make world class SB, and in some cases have succeeded. I feel like I see less of this ambition on the Pouilly-Fumé side of the river, which seems more content pumping out volumes of good quality/good price wine.

Side Note: I will exclude Dagueneau from the overt generalization of Pouilly-Fumé wine I made above. They make wine in both AOCs and both are considered some of the best, if not the best SB in the world.

Our recommendations:

Well, good luck finding any of the Dagueneau from the Sancerre side. That shit is difficult to come by. Small quantity, high demand. But their Pouilly-Fumé stuff is a bit more accessible, albeit not cheap. I like the Silex; it's got great minerality because it is grown in flint soils.

Didier Dagueneau Silex Pouilly-Fumé

On Sancerre side, we're gonna go with an old vines recommendation. I'm continuing to foreshadow my old vines rant that is coming at some point.

Patient Cottat Anciennes Vignes Sancerre

And here's a more affordable Pouilly-Fumé. Generally you can find great examples of this in the $25-35 range. Sancerre tends to be more in the $30-40 range for most solid producers.

Pascal Jolivet Pouilly-Fumé

Drink Well!

DRINKING & KNOWING THINGS
#39: SAUVIGNON BLANC PART 2

You may recall from last week that I said that I drink three different kinds of Sauvignon Blanc, for different reasons. It's like motorcycles. Sometimes I'm in the mood to take the Harley out and cruise around making lots of noise. Sometimes I want to tear through the canyons like a complete asshole, at which point the Aprilia is a better bet, and sometimes I like to look really fucking cool so I might go the Moto Guzzi route or maybe the Triumph.

Sauvignon Blanc is kind of similar. There's enough different expressions of this grape that you ought to be able to find something you're into. Hopefully all of you were able to track down a Pouilly-Fumé or a Sancerre last week and try a crisp refreshing Sauvignon Blanc from France. Hope you enjoyed that experience because we are gonna make a hard left turn here and go check out a completely different expression of SB also from France. In this case straight to Bordeaux.

I know a lot of you read that and were like WTF? Bordeaux? This is because Bordeaux has been really fucking good at branding for a long damn time, so when you hear the word Bordeaux you immediately associate it with the super expensive rated growth Châteaus like Château Lafite or Château Mouton-Rothschild where they produce big expressive red wines from Cabernet Sauvignon and Merlot which sell for thousands of dollars and they make movies like Sideways about them.

True, Bordeaux does produce those wines. But those only represent maybe 2-3% at best of the total volume of wines produced in that region. It's equivalent to mentioning Chevrolet and immediately saying, oh yeah, the sports car company that makes Corvettes. Yes, Chevy makes a few Corvettes every year, which are then highly coveted by paunchy middle-aged men with bad hair and worse jewelry who often wear too much Drakkar Noir (no offense, Maberry...it smells good on you.). But the vast majority of what Chevy produces is not sports cars or Corvettes. Same with Bordeaux. And the paunchy middle-aged analogy holds for Bordeaux as well...

> **Pro Tip:** As a stand-alone region, Bordeaux produces more volume of wine than the entire continent of Australia. A lot of it is inexpensive five-Euro-a-jug kind of wine.

Pretty much everyone is familiar with the red Bordeaux varietals. But what many people don't know is that Bordeaux also makes white wine, primarily from the SB grape. Not too surprising that the whites are less well known; only about 7-8% of the total Bordeaux production volume is white.

Why White Bordeaux is Dope AF:

They make two different styles of white Bordeaux. Let's call them "cheap" and "good". The cheap style is pretty similar to other cheap SB. Nothing special about these wines and in fact some of the shittiest wine I have ever had has been low end wines from Bordeaux. The "good" options are much more ambitious. These are typically a blend of SB and Semillon. Usually one of the two grapes is dominant in the blend, but they are Semillon dominant as often as they are SB dominant.

> **Pro Tip:** There's actually like five or six allowable grapes but pretty much everyone who makes a high-quality white Bordeaux sticks with SB and Semillon.
>
> **+1 Pro Tip:** The world renown Château Margaux produces a miniscule amount of white Bordeaux every year called Pavillon Blanc and it is 100% SB. No Semillon in the mix.
>
> **+2 Pro Tip:** 2020 is actually the 100th anniversary of Pavillon Blanc. This isn't important to know at all, it's a douchey little bit of wine trivia that I know and am telling you solely to emphasize how fucking smart I am.

The goal in Bordeaux is to make a rich, creamy textured wine. They accomplish this by fermenting the wine in barrels, and then allowing the wine to sit on the dead yeast (the lees) in the barrels for a few months, stirring it up now and then to make sure the wines get the full benefit of the flavor from the lees. The oak from the barrels adds structure and oak flavors to the wine, which also gives the wine the ability to age for a long time.

Side Note: Semillon makes a pretty neutral wine initially. But when Semillon ages, after about six or seven years it starts to develop this super amazing set of flavors like lanolin and honey, which makes it a great component in age-worthy white Bordeaux.

When done well, white Bordeaux is one of the best white wines in the world. But the rich, textured oaky style of Bordeaux is completely different from the grassy mineral wines of the Loire. And like the Bordeaux red wines, they are much better when they are ten years or more old, in marked contrast to the wines of the Loire which should be enjoyed when young and fresh.

White Bordeaux is an area where a price rule can be used with some degree of efficacy. First, pick up the bottle and make sure the wine is white, not red. This nuance should be readily apparent, even if you are from Texas. If the wine is under $20 it's probably the cheap style. Over $20 and you are getting into the good stuff (which can go up to $800-1000 a bottle for the really rare options).

Side Note: The cheap stuff isn't necessarily bad wine. It's just that a $12 bottle of white Bordeaux is not gonna be that different than a $12 bottle of any other SB. It's unremarkable.

Here's a great option of something good:
Château Pique Cailloux Blanc

But if you want to spend a bit more, this one is ridiculously great.

Château Cos d'Estournel Blanc

I said at the start of all this that I drink three types of SB, for different reasons. We come now to the third and final reason – which is trying to preserve my sanity whilst slogging through an endless swampland of chain restaurants and boring airport "wine bars" with the same four selections as last time.

The key here is New Zealand SB. Here's why.

Why New Zealand Sauvignon Blanc is Dope AF:

It's is the exact opposite of white Bordeaux. This is a crisp, zesty acidic wine and the green notes ('pyrazines" for the assholes) are so pronounced it's almost like biting into a fresh green bell pepper. (It's so obvious even Baby Mike can do it.) It's the Big Mac of wine. No matter who makes it – they are all going to be the same. You know exactly what you will get and it is totally tolerable.

> **Side Note:** There are some really high-quality standout SBs from New Zealand and I don't need eight hundred emails from different people explaining why their favorite Kiwi's stuff is totally different and unique. I am not knocking it. I am talking about the bulk of the export market – that $12-18 bottle of New Zealand SB.

Now, here's why this style is important. When New Zealand started making wine they couldn't get any cork, so they said fuck it, we are gonna make all our wines, even the most expensive and rare ones, with screw caps. Because all the producers went in together, the whole rest of the world was like "Alright, New Zealand gets a pass on having to use corks and their screw cap wines are great. But everybody else, fuck you, we still expect you to use corks, even though you'd have to be some kind of moron business owner to make a product that was protected by a closure that you knew had a 5-10% failure rate."

So now we have a wine that is cheap ($12-18) and is closed with a screw cap. This is the best of all possible options for restaurants, cafes, the fucking United Red Carpet club, hosted bars at weddings or conferences, everywhere in the world that serves wine by the glass. With a cork, whatever's left in the bottle at the end of the night is gonna go bad. With a screw cap you can easily pop the top back on and put it back in the fridge. Plus it's way faster to open when you have a line of people waiting.

This means you can get it everywhere. As I roll through life, I find myself all the time in places where I want a glass of wine. But all the weird shit I'm into is not available by the glass, and even if it is available by the bottle I don't want a whole bottle of Vin Jaune at three in the afternoon at the airport. I just want one glass.

And there's always a New Zealand SB by the glass available. It's always the same. I know exactly what I am going to get. It's a fresh enjoyable wine. And most importantly, I know I'm not going to despise it, which is not always the case when ordering wine by the glass.

There's no question that the wine I drink most by the glass is New Zealand SB. That said, I almost never buy bottles of it. I can honestly say in my entire cellar I don't have a single bottle of New Zealand SB. But it's a damn important wine to know about because until they make DAKT part of the mandatory K-12 curriculum in this country (feel free to contact your local congressperson to lobby for this and/or start petitions at Change.org) we are all going to have to continue living in a country that sucks at wine. New Zealand SB is going to be one of your primary survival mechanisms.

But if you're dying to get yourself a whole bottle, this is a kickass producer, and one of the finer examples of the milieu.

Cloudy Bay Marlborough Sauvignon Blanc

Glasses are available at gas stations and vending machines near you....

Drink Well!

DRINKING & KNOWING THINGS
#40: UPDAHG

One of the unbridled joys of being the World's Leading Wine Influencer is when I take a super obscure wine that I love and introduce you, the hoi polloi, to something special that you likely would never try on your own. Consequently, today we are going to talk about one of my favorite wines of all time – Updahg!

Now I realize that a lot of you are sitting there asking "what's Updahg" and I have only one response.

"Nuttin' much, s'up with you?"

Oh dear God I am sitting here typing this and laughing so hard snot is running down my face as I imagine Ann reading this and coming to the abrupt realization that I fucking got her again! She falls for this stupid joke every damn time and it is hilarious every time, but working it into a DAKT is a master stroke of literary genius. I just won at life....

That said, I assume that the rest of you are less amused with me than I am, which is okay. Not everyone is into cerebral humor. But I'll make it up to you by making good on my obscure wine promise and talk to you today about Lillet.

Why Lillet is Dope AF:

Lillet is part of a larger category of wine called aromatized wine. This is a bit of a unique category, and frankly some people do not consider these to be "wine". In fact, the Institute of Masters of Wine excludes aromatized wine from their overall consideration, and this category would not be included on any MW exams. The Guild of Master Sommeliers though might potentially include aromatized wines on portions of their exams. So who knows....

More importantly though, who cares about the academic categorization of these wines? Some are delicious and you should totally drink them.

To make an aromatized wine – first you make a relatively neutral dry wine, usually white. Then you dump some brandy into it to make it a fortified wine and crank the alcohol up (bonus!). Then, like Colonel Sanders, you add your secret blend of herbs and spices to the mix and steep that motherfucker in the herbs like a pot of Earl Grey for some period of time. Then you filter out the herbs and voilà – aromatized wine.

Some of you are sitting there thinking, wow, that sounds disgusting. It's like making Fernet Branca out of wine. And you wouldn't be all wrong. I've had some fairly nasty aromatized wines. Generally these are pretty rough to drink on their own, and typically find their place in cocktails (hmmm, wine cocktails...that probably deserves its own DAKT at some point).

Pro Tip: Aromatized wines are one of the oldest types of wine. No one really knows for sure, but it is highly likely that these wines served as medicine way back in the day. Also the herbs likely helped preserve the wines for a little while longer back when no one had Vinotemp coolers.

Many aromatized wines are fairly obscure smaller production kinds of wines, but there is at least one aromatized wine that you are all familiar with – Vermouth.

Yep, that's right. Your martinis are made with wine. Betcha most of you didn't know this.

Side Note: Because Vermouth is wine, it oxidizes and goes bad like any other wine will after you open it. The brandy and the herbs will preserve it a little bit longer, but my guess is that after about a week or so your Vermouth is gonna go bad. Which sucks because you only use a tiny bit when you make martinis, so either you are throwing away most of the bottle every time you make martinis or you are making shitty martinis with old Vermouth that has gone bad.

Pro Tip: If you are super into martinis, go down to BevMo and buy a boatload of the little airplane bottles of Vermouth. Problem solved.

If you've ever tried to drink a glass of straight Vermouth, you probably have a pretty good idea of why some people don't consider aromatized wine to be wine. (If you haven't tried it, I recommend that you pour yourself a nice tall glass of Vermouth and videotape yourself drinking it and then post it on social media so we can all have a good laugh at your expense.) However, there are some eminently drinkable options in this category. My favorite is Lillet Blanc (they also make a rosé and a red which IMHO are not as delicious).

Lillet Blanc has a lot of flowery aromatics; flavor-wise you'll get honey and candied citrus. This is a pretty full-bodied wine (they make a reserve Lillet Blanc as well which is even better). It's one of only a few aromatized wines that IMHO you can sit back and drink a glass of. However, where it really is spectacular is in Lillet tonics. Super easy recipe. Put Lillet in a glass with ice, tonic water and a lime. Think of it as a gin and tonic that doesn't have the shitty bitter taste of gin but flowery honey instead. This is one of the all-time greatest pool drinks. Also, Lillet is like 17% percent alcohol instead of the 40%+ in gin so you can drink three times as many Lillet tonics as gin and tonics.

I would put a link in here, but Lillet Blanc is available basically everywhere. So next time you're at the grocery store or the liquor store, search it out and make some Lillet tonics. You'll lose your goddamn mind.

Just remember that Lillet is wine. Finish the bottle in a couple of days or it's gonna turn brown and go bad.

Drink Well!!

Drinking & Knowing Things
#41: SPATBURGUNDER

I receive tons of emails from devoted DAKT followers each week. Most of the time they are the sycophantic kind where they inform me how much they love DAKT, or how DAKT changed their life, or marriage proposals, or sonnets composed to celebrate the wisdom of the World's Leading Wine Influencer, or Erik complaining about how Sweden is continually represented.

I read every single one of these because I am a rabid egomaniac who is solely dependent on the adulation and adoration of others to bolster my poor self-esteem.

No, I'm joking of course. I never read the ones from Erik.

The other types of emails I get are from people who offer suggestions about what wine(s) they want to see highlighted in DAKTs. These generally go unread by me because a) those people aren't the World's Leading Wine Influencer so their wine opinions are meaningless and b) often they are for shitty wines that don't meet our rigid Dope AF standard. Also I am generally an asshole.

That said, I received a couple of requests/suggestions the last couple of weeks which I think I can wrap together and also get to a potential Dope AF recommendation. Specifically, Video Jill was whinging about wanting more reds in the mix because now it is fall, and Chuck was suggesting that we do something German because, you know, Oktoberfest. (Feel free to insert your own sarcastic comment here around Oktoberfest being all about beer and not wine....)

But I think I can put these together and talk about Spatburgunder.

Why Spatburgunder is Dope AF:

Spatburgunder is what the Germans call Pinot Noir. So there you are. We have already established beyond a shadow of a doubt that Pinot Noir is Dope AF. That said, many places around the world produce Pinot Noir, and few of them are consistently Dope AF. Germany is no exception.

> **Pro Tip:** Germany is the world's third largest producer of Pinot Noir. More than Australia and New Zealand combined.

Historically, the Spatburgunder coming out of Germany was sort of meh at best. Pinot Noir is a fickle grape to work with, and typically likes cooler climates. Germany for many years was more focused on even cooler climate grapes, like Riesling, which gets barely ripe enough in some areas to make wine, and consequently the Spatburgunder was pretty uninteresting at best. But then a few things happened.

First, climate change occurred. Grape growing regions started to get warmer in Germany, which opened up more opportunities to grow different varieties. Secondly, more winemakers realized that Germany was able to grow some pretty damn good Pinot Noir grapes, and these wines generally have a higher price point than lesser known grapes like Muller-Thurgau or Silvaner. So winemakers shifted their mindsets towards making a more ambitious style of Pinot Noir; one with increased complexity and ageability.

> **Side Note:** This climate change stuff is really impacting certain wine regions like Champagne, which has been super successful by being on the very margin of acceptable climates for grape growing. This is freaking out a bunch of the large Champagne houses, who have responded to this by buying up land in England to grow Champagne grapes in. Typically England has been too cold, but the soil there is the same chalky Kimmeridgian soil as in Champagne, so as the world continues to heat up like a Crock Pot set on low people believe that we'll probably shift Champagne production to England at some point. This will be amusing given the fanaticism around Champagne and if you know anything about the history between France and England.

> **+1 Side Note:** This soil is why the White Cliffs of Dover are white.

+2 Side Note: They're already producing some pretty awesome sparkling wines in England, particularly in Sussex and Kent – so keep an eye out for those at your local wine shop and give them a try if you like Champagne.

Back to Germany, where these factors are working together to create an ecosystem where some damn good Pinot Noirs are emerging. I'll call these in some cases as acceptable alternatives to Premier Cru Burgundy, although I've yet to see anything that truly rivals the Grand Crus of Burgundy.

But who cares? It's kickass Pinot Noir but because it is labeled Spatburgunder and it comes from Germany it's going to be way cheaper than the equivalent quality Burgundy.

Side Note: The best Spatburgunder I ever had I drank at a little restaurant on a canal on the outskirts of Berlin and it was like forty Euros in the restaurant. I figured that meant it was probably about a twenty Euro retail price point so I checked around in other wine stores for it but came up empty handed. It was spectacular.

The point is there are some real gems coming out of Germany for the Pinot Noir lovers. This comes with a caveat however. I think some of these producers are trying to make a recipe wine – i.e. a wine that meets certain style and taste parameters that they think will sell in the US, rather than trying to express the German terroir in their Spatburgunder. Which brings up an interesting pricing dynamic. What I see is that in some cases, the Spatburgunder at the top of the market (say above $60) is more often than not a recipe wine, and is likely to be overoaked and overextracted. And the Spatburgunder that is below say $20 a bottle is the less ambitious fruitier style; more of a picnic wine than a serious Pinot Noir.

So we are going to look for wines that fall within those two price boundaries. The ones we want will also be labeled with the normal confusing German wine labels as opposed to Americanizing them with more English descriptors. This way we'll have a pretty good feeling that these wines are made by a winemaker who is really trying to emphasize the German terroir for Germans as opposed to making a recipe wine for Americans.

Side Note: One of the worst Pinot Noirs I ever had was in Cochem, Germany, where we had been drinking Riesling for days and were desperate for something red. I bought the only thing I could find, which was like an eight Euro bottle of Spatburgunder and it tasted like Hawaiian Punch and rubbing alcohol. We poured the bottle out; just couldn't get through it. So we gotta tread carefully when trying Spatburgunder.

+1 Side Note: I think there is a very real possibility that in twenty years or so some of the Spatburgunders are going to be as sought after and coveted as Grand Cru Burgundy and won't you look like a genius if you have a few cases laid down somewhere aging, like the folks who grabbed up DRC in the 1980s.

+2 Side Note: The picnic style is not for aging. You're gonna look like a moron if you have a couple of cases of that stuff laid down.

On to our recommendations, which for Spatburgunder are pretty damn tough. There are so many different climates across the thirteen German wine regions and so many different soil types that it is hard to really put a specific "style" on Spatburgunder. Then add in the normal confusing German wine labels with their Trockens and their Grosses Gewachs and Erste Lages and that makes it worse. So I don't have great direction to give you all except to try things from different areas and regions. As long as you stay within the price boundaries above you'll probably have a pretty good experience. And when you find stuff you like, grab a case and stash it somewhere for a while, because the prices on these are going to continue rising.

You can start with this one...

Weingut Dautel Spatburgunder

Drink Well!!

Drinking & Knowing Things
#42: A TALE OF TWO MONTEPULCIANOS

Ok, let's acknowledge that one of the largest impediments to becoming a functional wine geek is the goddamn complexity of wine, particularly in Europe. I'm not criticizing this. I completely understand that one little town has been calling its favorite grape "Cot" for hundreds of years, while the next town over calls the same grape "Auxerrois", and the town after that calls it "Jacobian", and the next town calls it "Prunelat". Then some asshole scientist discovers that all the grapes are genetically the same and decrees that it be called "Malbec" and people say "Fuck That" and keep labeling their wine like they have done for hundreds of years. That's fair. It just makes it more difficult for us, the DAKT team, to suss out what is worth drinking.

It also is why wine is interesting. Unpacking this stuff takes time and effort. Fortunately, I am drinking tirelessly on your behalf.

So Europe is complicated, from a wine perspective. German wine labels are borderline incomprehensible. France has a bunch of different systems (e.g. in Bordeaux they rate the winery, while in Burgundy they rate the individual vineyards.).

But the most confusing of all has got to be Italy. I feel like Italy is fractally difficult. You could take any slice of it (grape, region, style etc) and pop the hood on it and each individual component would be as complicated, if not more complicated than the entire thing.

This makes it simultaneously frustrating and fun. You could spend an entire lifetime studying Italian wine and still not even get through part of it. We're not gonna do that, because we have a whole world of wine to drink through. But we'll hit some of the bigger parts of Italy. Today we are gonna cover Montepulciano.

Why Montepulciano is Dope AF:
Well, that depends on which Montepulciano you are talking about. There's two major ones and they are quite different. Knowing Italy there are probably seventeen other Montepulcianos in play as well, but we are only gonna talk about the two major ones.

Vino Nobile De Montepulciano:
In Tuscany, they make a boatload of Sangiovese. The vast majority of these wines are labeled as Chianti or Chianti Classico. But there are two small towns located within the Chianti region, and their wines are considered to be special enough to have their own names for the Sangiovese produced there. One of these wines you have heard of: Brunello di Montalcino, or simply "Brunello". The other is Vino Nobile de Montepulciano ("Noble Wine from Montepulciano"), or often just "Vino Nobile". These are both considered higher quality expressions of Sangiovese, and the rules for these wines are a bit more stringent. Now, I love Sangiovese, but my favorite is Vino Nobile. A lot of the wines labeled Chianti or Chianti Classico can be more volume-based wine at lower price points. It's fine, but often nothing spectacular. Brunello can be absolutely fantastic, but it is a) expensive and b) often has so much oak treatment that it needs ten years or so aging to really enter the sweet spot.

Vino Nobile, conversely, often has less oak so is more approachable without lots of aging. More importantly, it is way cheaper than the equivalent quality Brunello – often less than half the price. If I am going to drink Sangiovese my go-to is almost always Vino Nobile. My local Pavilions sells one off the grocery shelf for like $19 and I get it all the time.

So if you like Chianti or Brunello do yourself a solid and spend a few more bucks and pick up a Vino Nobile de Montepulciano. Here's a great option for under $30.

Maria Caterina Dei Vino Nobile di Montepulciano

But we aren't here today to talk about Sangiovese. We are all about the weird stuff. Which brings us to Montepulciano number two – in this case the grape, not the town.

In southern Italy, directly east from Rome, is a region called Abruzzo. The Rockstar grape in Abruzzo is a grape called "Montepulciano" (not to be confused with the town "Montepulciano" in Tuscany). They produce a range of wines from this grape – from deeper complex ageworthy wines to lower complexity picnic wines. Most of these will be labeled Montepulciano d'Abruzzo ("Montepulciano from Abruzzo").

Pro Tip: Believe it or not, Montepulciano is one of the most exported Italian wines by volume. This is mostly due to the picnic style, which you can grab all day long at your local Trader Joes for $9.

We aren't necessarily after those wines though. We are after the big, bold powerful ageable wines. Flavorwise, Montepulciano is a deep red wine, with great spice, herbal and pepper notes.

Side Note: I had heard about how great Montepulciano could be, but at the time I didn't believe it. I had only had the picnic style, and I thought it was ok, but nothing to make your socks roll up and down. Then I was with Lyin' Bidet Yo and some ladies in southern Italy, and I made a point out of searching out the older more complex versions of this wine. Mind blown. Now whenever I look at Italian wine lists or catalogues I always have an eye out for some of the bigger Montepulciano-based wines because in my mind they can rival the Barolos and Brunellos of the world. I specifically look for ones with fifteen years or more of age on them. Plus they will be super cheap, comparatively.

+1 Side Note: Just to keep it confusing, legally you can also blend in up to 15% Sangiovese with Montepulciano. Makes me wonder if you sourced those Sangiovese grapes from the town of Montepulciano if you could legally call the wine Montepulciano d'Abruzzo de Montepulciano. Probably not...

I keep referring to this wine as Montepulciano d'Abruzzo. But there are some subzones which are allowed to label their wine differently, like

Colline Teramane (which even the casual observer should note does not contain the word Montepulciano in it – you have to know.) But this is some super esoteric wine geekiness. If you stick with wines labeled Montepulciano d'Abruzzo you should be fine.

This is another area where we want to use a price rule, given the range of quality coming out of here. Stick with wines that are over $15 if you want the complex style. If you get over $40 you should be getting into the real gems – wines that would likely cost over $100 if they were Brunello or Barolo. Note that if you want a nice daily drinker you can find acceptable quality Montepulciano under $10 all day long. Just don't expect anything spectacular other than the price.

Another quick tip to look for is anything labeled "Riserva". These have more stringent quality requirements.

For our recommendations – there's a bunch of the lower priced options – and I encourage you to grab a couple to get a sense of what a ten-dollar bottle of wine could be. These will blow away most of your domestic ten-dollar bottles. Here's one.

Carletto Montepulciano d'Abruzzo

But getting into the real legit options will require a bit more digging.

Orlandi Contucci Montepulciano d'Abruzzo Colline Teramane

If you are the kind of person who likes laying things down for a while these big Montepulcianos can age a very long time. I have had some from the 1970s which have still been vibrant and delicious. Toss a case in the back of your closet and wait ten years...

Drink Well!!

Drinking & Knowing Things
#43: WINE RATINGS DECIPHERED

Wine ratings are complete bullshit.

I was going to stop after that sentence, because that is all you need to know. But I recognize that some of you may need a bit more convincing. If that's you, feel free to read on. Everyone else can quit now and go open up a bottle of something interesting.

Let's separate wine ratings into two separate categories.

Ratings assigned to specific wines by critics whose job it is to rate wines.

Online ratings like Vivino or Amazon or whatever that are consumer driven.

Both are complete bullshit. Don't pay any attention to them. Here's why:

Why Ratings Assigned By Critics Are Bullshit:
The ratings assigned by critics generally use a one hundred point scale. These are the ones you hear people bragging about e.g. "this wine got ninety-seven points".

This system was brought into focus by Robert Parker, and has been adopted by Wine Spectator, Wine Enthusiast, James Suckling, Antonio Galloni and others.

In fact though, it isn't a one hundred point scale. Some critics only score between eighty and one hundred points, while others score from fifty to one hundred. Which means you can't even reasonably compare ratings from two different critics on the same bottle. And no one ever scores anything below fifty points. So it might as well be a twenty-point scale or whatever.

"Well, why don't you just make it a twenty-point scale?"

Best Nigel Tufnel voice: "This one goes to a hundred..."

Moreover, the reality is that you never really see any ratings advertised below about eighty-eight points, and the vast majority of wines that do advertise their ratings are between eighty-eight and ninety-two points. (Don't believe me? Check next time you are at BevMo or Total Wine or your grocery store. If you can find a rating under eighty-eight points take a photo and post it and tag @drinkingandknowing.)

Which ostensibly means it really is a five-point scale, with a few standouts that get some higher scores.

So the numbers themselves become pretty much meaningless. Why then all the fuss about wines that are rated ninety-nine or one hundred point wines? These are wines that critics have determined are the best of the best and you should buy them immediately. Except that when you get to these kinds of ratings you are guessing. Here's why:

Wines that are thought of as being the highest possible quality generally have a great deal of complexity and ageability. But you can't wait twenty years to decide whether or not a Bordeaux is high quality. The critics taste it often before release, out of the barrel. Then, because they are soooooo good and soooooo smart, they decide that it is a one-hundred-point wine based on what they think it is going to evolve into eventually, even though it is basically undrinkable at the time.

Pro Tip: No one is consistently that good. Except maybe me.

The next big issue is that wine ratings often look at the archetype for a particular wine and use that as the benchmark. In other words, I know that Bordeaux should show black currant, and pencil lead, and vanilla. So if someone is hypothetically making an Bordeaux Rosé with lots of floral notes, that wine could be spectacular, but it would likely get crappy ratings because it isn't an archetypal Bordeaux.

Side Note: Just for shits and giggles I went online to see if I could find a Bordeaux Rosé and what the corresponding ratings were. I found one that came in at eighty-nine points from wine critic Wilfred Wong (hmm, between eighty-eight and ninety-two points – shocking…). What I don't know is if Wilfred thought this bottle wasn't that great, but had rated a bunch of other Bordeaux Rosés in the high nineties. I doubt it but who knows. My sample of one is not statistically significant.

Another issue is that every critic's palate and preferences are different. Robert Parker is a great example of this. He liked lots of oak, so wines that showed higher oak treatment got higher scores from him. Producers responded by using more oak just to get higher scores from him. Today there is a company in Napa that uses a computer algorithm to analyze wine to inform producers what they need to add or do in order to achieve specific scores.

As a die-hard capitalist, I applaud this as a sales and marketing strategy and I don't fault producers for doing this. That's the game, at least in the US (just one more way we screwed up wine here). And I can't wait to start gaming the system when our Bhutan wine starts getting rated.

As a Wineaux though it offends me. My biggest hope for all of us is that wine producers would start making the best possible wine they can out of whatever the harvest gives them from their terroir, and not manipulating the hell out of it just to get one more point in the next issue of Wine Spectator.

Side Note: When SoCal Rum got a ninety-five point rating – the highest ever awarded to a light rum – we marketed the hell out of that. So either I am a total hypocrite or a genius marketer. Probably it is more that I can't change the game overnight so I might as well win under the current rules…

An approach that some of my wine friends use is to find a critic whose palate and preferences are reasonably similar to their own, and just rely on that person's ratings. This strategy has some validity, but falls down because many critics often specialize in only one region or type of wine, e.g. Burgundy or Italy. Which is fine if all you ever want to drink is Burgundy, but we don't want that. We want to drink the whole world of wine.

Another major issue with ratings is that the vast majority (probably 90%+) of wines don't get rated. For example, last night I had a Cab Franc from Slovenia. It was fucking awesome. But no one is going to take the time to bother rating a Slovenian Cab Franc because it isn't marketed at volume and is completely unknown. And I am all about finding the wines that no one knows about and are awesome, because they are also inexpensive.

Next, let's get to the fact that YOUR palate and preferences are a) specific to you and b) hopefully evolving and changing as you try more types of wine. Just because someone else thinks it is good in no way, shape or form means you will like it. I'm sure some of you who tried the Vin Jaune from DAKT #32 can attest to that.

Side Note: Most of you loved it, I know. But we gotta be patient with the newbies and Oregonians...

The bottom line is don't listen to the critics. Listen to yourself. Critics' ratings at this point are basically a marketing tool. And it's idiotic. We don't rate food i.e. look, this loaf of Sourdough got ninety-two points, while this loaf of Rye only got ninety points. Apples from this farmer got eighty-eight points, while this other guy got ninety. It's absurd. And even if we did rate food, you would still buy the Rye bread or the Washington apple if that was what you were into. You wouldn't even consider the ratings.

Why the Vivino Style Ratings Are Bullshit:
Next, let's examine the Vivino style rating system, where all the consumers rate wines by one to four stars or one to five stars or whatever on an app or the internet. This is crowd sourcing; law of averages. This should tell us what people actually think about the wine.

Except it doesn't. Here's why:
First off you are now relying on the palates of everybody. We have already established that "everybody" is not always "good at wine", which is why DAKT exists in the first place. In fact, the vast majority are not very good at discerning whether or not a wine is high quality. Moreover, people's

preferences are different. Some people are going to greatly enjoy a wine that objectively isn't very complex or ageable. Here's a perfect example of what the crowd thinks of a very inexpensive wine:

https://www.amazon.com/Apothic-Red-Blend-750-ml/product-reviews/B005J78A2O

And what I usually see is that no one ever takes time to rate a wine they think is average. People are only going to take the time to do a review or enter a rating if they either really like or love something or really hate it. So what you end up with for every single wine is a bunch of fours and fives and a handful of ones, and they all average out to somewhere between three point seven and four point four stars (on a five point scale).

Don't believe me? Go on Amazon or Vivino or wine.com and try to find any wine with statistically significant accuracy (say over fifty ratings) that is below three point five or above four point six stars.

Then let's add in that producers are then incentivized to manipulate the system (e.g. walk into a tasting room and see how often you'll see a discount offered if you post a Trip Advisor review).

Thus, the crowd-sourced ratings become meaningless as everything regresses to the mean.

I once developed an algorithm that I think would fix this entire wine rating problem, as well as having applicability to all types of wine (true story). It was way too much trouble to implement, however, so instead I developed this simple system that I recommend you all adopt immediately. If we do our jobs right we can change the world.

This system is one you all know already. It is:

Is the wine Dope AF?

If yes, drink it. If not, don't.

"Yes, Mike, but how will we know if the wine is Dope AF?"

Well, besides from me telling you, which is probably the most expeditious and effective method – your basic strategy should be the Paul Grieco approach:

Take a sip. If it makes you want another, take another. If that makes you want a whole glass, drink that. Keep on going until you decide to stop.

If you stop after a few sips, the wine is likely not Dope AF.

I will add a small caveat here which is to not rely solely on a single data point to conclude. There's always bottle variation, and storage/shipping issues, and differences between producers in a certain area or vintage. Then there is also the issue of your evolving palate. Like the Tannat in DAKT #9, you may find that wines you didn't like two years ago may now be Dope AF for you.

So keep after it. Ignore the critics. Ignore the marketing idiots. Ignore the wisdom of the masses. Trust your palate. If you try a ninety-nine-point wine and hate it, be comfortable saying so as candidly as you want.

And Drink Well!!

p.s. Also stop bragging about the ninety-seven-point wine you recently bought that you can't drink for fifteen years. No one gives a shit. I'd much rather hear about the Slovenian Cab Franc you tried, and either loved or hated, and why.

DRINKING & KNOWING THINGS
#44: WHITE RIOJA

I'm gonna grab the mic, and start to flow and show ya
A Dope AF delicious wine that's known as White Rioja
And here's a bit of knowledge that's really gonna rock ya
Those crazy Europeans all pronounce it White Ree-Ock-Ah

It's like a regular Rioja except it's an albino
You gotta know this shit if you're gonna be a Wineaux
Relax and grasp a glass and let the Maestro learn ya
The variety with notoriety that's known as Viura

(There are other local grapes allowed, it's true, but no one cares
By law big dog Viura comprises more than half the share.)

It's obscure, to be sure, and production's Lilliputian
And here in the US we get fuck all distribution
A search for it often frustrates like finding Waldo
So when I see some on a shelf I snag it *muy pronto*

I can hear a whiny Swedish voice asking if it's Dope AF
I'm about to spit enlightenment so buckle the fuck up
Here we must tread cautiously so we don't make a bungle
There are two types – where one's complex the other's very humble

The difference tween the twain is the latter's young or *"joven"*
It's not complex and I must stress it's very easygoing
But what we want is textures, layers and some nuance
And balance where the elements all sing in congruence

So on our quest to find the best we look for style two
As a DAKT disciple you'll know exactly what to do
The key to understanding is apparent on the label
The words will be in Spanish but you don't need to be bilingual

What we want is wines labeled Reserva or Gran Reserva
If it isn't either one of those, then Broham keep on searching
These reign supreme, serious juice that's seen a lot of aging
Nab a case and a *porron* and get the party raging

"Maestro," she inquired. "What makes these wines so special?"
Just shut your mouth and listen, and then keep it confidential
I must confess that its success is lots of oxidation
And on that shit I must admit I have a strange fixation

Reservas age for two long years with six months in a barrel
The wine develops character, like 1980's Perry Farrell
Gran Reservas age twice as long, I'm happy to inform ya
Aged inside a proper cask not some dumb hipster amphora

(The really good producers all exceed these legal limits
Eight or ten years aging is a typical exhibit.)

If you like your white wine crisp and clean, with linear precision
Do not attempt this wine at home without proper supervision
Cause this wine is formidable, and it might give you angst or
Intimidate, unless you roll straight up Wineaux gangster.

Flavorwise you'll recognize the wine is pretty neutral
If you seek floral aromatics then your search will not be fruitful
Expect to find inside this wine lots of nutty goodness
If White Rioja was a beer it'd prolly be a Guinness

It has a deep distinctive hue, like a Mason jar of urine
It tastes fanfuckingtastic, though some find the sight disturbing

Although it's bold, it also holds noticeable acidity
So with a bone of aged *jamon* it has a great affinity

If you're inclined to try this wine, please proceed with prudence
Inform the greenhorn at the store you know a guy with influence
And if they don't have some in stock, tell them to go to hell
Then seek it out some other place so you can all Drink Well!!

(Chances are in your locale, this wine will be a bitch to locate
So here's a link to make it quick for all you lazy Snowflakes.)
Lopez de Heredia Vina Tondonia Blanco Reserva

Drinking & Knowing Things
#45: THANKSGIVING EDITION

Gotcha, suckers. Nope, I'm not doing a Thanksgiving edition. You all have enough knowledge now to pick out some interesting stuff and see what happens. Also every douchey whiney wine writer does this, which is why they are not the World's Leading Wine Influencer. But if you're dying for recommendations, go back and re-read DAKT 18: Sparkling Shiraz.

Today we're gonna try to make sense of WTF is a Super Tuscan? Time for a history lesson.

In Europe, every wine region has very specific rules about what you can put in a bottle and label it with the name of the region, e.g. Vouvray must be Chenin Blanc. In some cases the rules are a bit more broad, and in others they are very draconian down to limiting the pounds of grapes you can harvest per hectare, minimum alcohol levels and specificity on percentages in blends.

This is what happened in Tuscany. You all know the main region there which is Chianti. In order to have a wine labelled Chianti, it must be Sangiovese based (although you can mix in small percentages of other allowable grapes, even white grapes). But the dominant grape must be Sangiovese. Now, most people hear Tuscany and think about Florence and rolling hills and castles, which is all true. But Tuscany rolls down to the ocean, and has a shitload of maritime influence near the coast.

Pro Tip: There actually used to be a law that you had to put some white wine into the Chianti blend because there was a glut of white there. But winemakers bitched and finally they relaxed it. You can put in white grapes now, but you don't have to.

Back in the 1940s one of the winemakers there wanted to plant Cab Franc. He knew if he did he wouldn't be able to legally sell the wine as Tuscan wine, since it didn't meet the legal requirements. He said "fuck it" and did it anyway, and made the wine for himself to drink. Which alone is Dope AF.

Fast forward to the late 1960s/early 1970s and people started to realize that Bordeaux varietals grew super well in Tuscany, particularly as you got nearer to the ocean. So a handful of folks all said "fuck it" and started planting Cab, Merlot, Cab Franc and others. But there was no legal way to market the wine as anything particular, since there were no rules for Bordeaux varietals in Tuscany. Instead, they had to market it as simple table wine, even though it was anything but.

A few of these like Sassacaia, Ornellaia and Antinori 's Tignanello became highly coveted and sought after and started demanding huge price premiums. This of course made more people take notice, and more Bordeaux varietals got planted, and more volume erupted in the marketplace. There was no real way to describe these wines, so some old school influencer (not me, I was like ten years old and was only maybe a Middle School Influencer at best) called them a "Super Tuscan" and the name stuck.

Today, there is a huge sprawl of these wines at all price levels. Italy finally got off its ass and created a legal area for some of them which allows the wines to be labeled as Bolgheri. Some folks opted in on this, but many didn't as Bolgheri was completely unknown. Also they were used to having this fuck the rules attitude, which is totally punk rock and worthy of respect. So you'll never find anything labeled "Super Tuscan". That's just a made up name. The wine will be labeled either Bolgheri, or maybe IGT Toscano or maybe Vino da Tavola (table wine).

Why Super Tuscans are Dope AF:

If you like Bordeaux, you'll dig Super Tuscans. You'll get all the flavor profiles of Bordeaux, but the fruit will be a bit riper and you'll get these pretty big wines. A lot of producers are pretty heavy handed with the use of oak, so like Bordeaux these are wines that need some age on them, particularly the higher end ones.

However, the space is pretty crowded with producers these days. The original Fuck It guys are still grinding along and making great wines but the prices have gone through the roof, in some cases even eclipsing some of the highest rated Bordeaux wines (Masseto for example sells for around $750 a bottle). And the bottom end of the market is flooded with people cranking out overextracted juice and throwing wood chips in it.

But there are some real gems in here. What we are looking for are the wines that are Bordeaux-esque, made by smaller lesser known producers who are trying to make great wine as opposed to marketable wine. While you can drop five hundred smacks on one of Angelo Gaja's single vineyard wines, you can also drop forty bucks on something that is basically as good. That way you can get a case as opposed to a single bottle, which means you can host a Roman-style bacchanalia for you and three friends and still maybe have some wine left over for breakfast the next day.

This is an area where unfortunately you are gonna have to know some producers, because as previously mentioned you're not really gonna be able to tell what it is by the label. Some of the time they will list the blend on the label; other times not so much.

Side Note: One of the Tuscan blends that seems to be growing in volume is a Sangiovese/Cabernet Sauvignon blend. When I first heard about this I was like "yuck, that sounds horrific". Being open-minded and curious though I gave them a try and was super surprised at how enjoyable they are. My bad for being a judgmental asshole. I'm not sure how many times I need to learn this lesson, but apparently it is a lot.

On to our recommendations:

The first is a great example of a very traditional Bordeaux blend right in the sweet spot for pricing.

Tenute Argentiera Villa Donoratico Bolgheri

Our second recommendation is something a bit different, but is a trick I use a lot. Many of the high end wineries that produce Bordeaux blends offer a second label. These generally are the exact same grapes that go into the flagship wine, but for whatever reason the winemaker decided it didn't quite meet the standard to go into the main blend. Maybe that barrel evolved a little differently, or that batch came from newer vines and wasn't as complex, or they had a bit left over at the end or whatever. The wine is still great, but not quite perfect. They still bottle it up though and sell it under a second label. Basically the same wine, much lower price.

Side Note: Stay tuned for a DAKT on Bordeaux itself. That's where this little gambit will really come into play.

+1 Side Note: Everyone knows Opus. Opus does this and sells a second wine called Overture. Back in the day, you could only get it at the winery, and only if they had some in stock that year. Every time I would go to Napa I would swing by Opus and see if they had any Overture, which was $20 a bottle and I would load up the trunk. This was the best kept secret in Napa. Now unfortunately the secret is out and Overture now sells commercially for like $150 or more. Bastards!!

+2 Side Note: This is why you can't tell anyone about the secret stuff you learn in DAKT, because it fucks it up for everyone.

Anyway, this next recommendation is for the second label wine produced by Ornellaia (one of the original Fuck It crew), and is about one-third the price of the flagship wine. Get some in ya!

<u>Ornellaia Le Serre Nuove</u>

Drink Well!

DRINKING & KNOWING THINGS
#46: PORT

I've been getting tons of feedback from people about which DAKT wines they have liked. Seems like big crowd pleasers have been the Timorasso (shocker) and the Passetoutgrains (again, shocker).

I also got some weird Swedish feedback but I don't know what it means. If anyone can help translate "Du är min personliga hjälte och jag vill vara precis som du förutom att min penis är för liten" please let me know.

Today we're gonna lean in on a bit of a polarizing wine – Port. Some people love it; others think it is only suitable for elderly tweed-laden British gentlemen. I get it. It's high alcohol (bonus!) and also sweet. That's not for everyone. I would argue however, that those of you who claim to not like Port haven't had a good one. Not surprising, there's a swamp of crappy Port out there and also a lot of confusing options. As usual, I'll be your spirit guide to lead you through the morass of garbage and show you how to drink Port the right way. You won't even need any tweed.

Why Port is Dope AF:
Not all of it is. The question probably should be "which Ports are Dope AF". Let's break Port down into a few simple categories and rules:

Port from countries that are not Portugal but are labeled "Port" – Avoid these.

White Port – Do not under any circumstances drink this ever.

Pink Port – The only real possible use for this is in a cocktail called a Pink Lady, which is a pretty shitty cocktail at best. This is gonna be a hard pass as well.

Red Port – Some of these are spectacular. But like Indiana Jones, you must choose wisely or your face might melt.

Tawny Port – For the most part these will all be relatively drinkable, with some amazing standouts that probably represent one of the best values in aged wines.

Let's explore.

Port comes from the Douro Valley in Portugal, near the town of Oporto. It's made from a blend of local varietals. Up to like maybe a hundred different varietals are allowed but most people use the five major ones, with Touriga Nacional typically being the main one.

Since you are all DAKT Disciples, there's no need for me to go into how complicated the vineyard rating system in Portugal is. You all remember this from DAKT 29: Touriga, which I'm sure you have read and re-read numerous times, and perhaps have inked extracts of it on your forearm in one of those moronic millennial quote tattoos. (Feel free to post photos of those and tag @drinkingandknowing so we can all mock you.)

Port is super complicated, but I'll simplify it as much as I can. Pretty much all the Port production starts out the same. They dump all the grapes into giant concrete troughs and then either foot tread them with teams that lock arms and sing all day whilst stomping around like members of GWAR or smash them with these robot machines with a bunch of little feet that tread the grapes (Skynet has to start somewhere...). The juice starts fermenting, they dump in a ton of brandy to kill the yeast, and voilà, we have Port. Sweet, because there's still sugar left in the mix, and high alcohol because of the brandy.

Side Note: They do also make some dry and off-dry styles but the vast majority are sweet.

Here's where shit starts to diverge.

The crappiest of these wines are simply bottled up and sold as "ruby Port" or your basic red Port. You can find this at any wine store for $8-10 a bottle. It's harsh and also really extracted. It'll get you fucked up, for sure, but in an ugly way.

The better juice they dump into barrels and let age for a couple of years to see how they develop and evolve and then they start making some calls. At this point there are two options. If the vintage was a really great year, they pull it out, bottle it up and call it a Vintage Port. This happens two or three times a decade. These are the ones that get the hundred-point scores (for all you score whores). Here's the problem. These wines have been yanked out of the barrels while they are still young. They are meant to age very very slowly in the bottle. Vintage Port starts to become eminently drinkable after thirty years, but fifty or more years is generally even better. But everyone buys these Vintage Ports because of the scores and then immediately drinks them. Big fucking mistake. If you are going to buy a Vintage Port, either look for older ones (which can be bought typically pretty inexpensively – it's not hard to find one that is thirty years old for $80-100, which is about what you would pay for a current release), or buy a current release and stick it in your cellar for another twenty years.

Sometimes they don't have enough demand for Vintage in a particular year to bottle everything, or it doesn't evolve quite as well as they want it to so they let it age in the barrel for a few more years. Then it's bottled up and sold as Late Bottled Vintage Port or "LBV". These are generally fairly high quality, but cheaper than the Vintage options and are more approachable much sooner because they have spent an extra two or three years in a barrel. If I am going to a party and want to swing by the store to grab some Port to bring, an LBV is a great option because it can be drunk that night (although it too will benefit from some further bottling aging).

They don't bottle everything as Vintage or LBV though. Some of it they just leave in the barrel and let it keep aging. After about six or seven years in a barrel, the wine starts to turn brown. This is how they make Tawny Port. However, with the Tawny style they take a slightly different approach. With the Tawny, they keep aging it for forever, and occasionally pull some out of different barrels and blend it all together. When they do this they kind of guess the average age, although it is pretty loosey-goosey. The wines will be sold as either ten-year, twenty-year, thirty-year or forty-year Tawny Ports.

These are where you can find some really great stuff. I tend to stay away from the ten-year, because I think they grab a barrel of ten-year and mix it in with a bunch of stuff that is six or seven years old just to get it to market quickly. These are pretty inexpensive; you can get a ten-year Tawny for probably $15. The twenty and thirty-year versions are what I typically go after, particularly the thirty-year. The forty-year options are much harder to find and are generally pretty pricey. With a thirty-year, you can get something that is really great without breaking the bank.

Flavor-wise, the red ports (Vintage and LBV) will be fruit driven, dark berry, full bodied wines. The Tawny Ports will be very different, more caramel and dried fruit and nuts. Both can be great, it's just a matter of preference.

> **Pro Tip:** There are a shitload of other versions of Port that will be labeled things like Crusted, Colheita, Garrafeira, Reserve, etc. Don't worry about all this. Your basic rule should be:

If you want the fruit style and you want to drink it tonight, get an LBV or an older Vintage.

If you want to have cool stuff in your cellar, get Vintage and lay it down.

If you want the more nutty caramel version, get a twenty or thirty-year old Tawny.

Follow these and you will never go wrong. You're welcome!

And some recommendations for each:

Here's a link to a Vintage from Fonseca which is a really high-quality producer.

Fonseca Vintage Port

> **Side Note:** You can see the different vintages available from various resellers on www.wine-searcher.com. When I was copying this link I noticed they had one from 1920, which I clicked on just to check it out. $800 for a hundred year old Vintage Port. That's pretty dope.

Here's a great option for an LBV. I love Niepoort. Solid all day for $20.

Niepoort Late Bottled Vintage Port

And a 20 Year Tawny from a classic producer.

Taylor Fladgate Twenty Year Tawny Port

And if for whatever reason you can't fathom enjoying Port without some tweed, here's one of my favorite producers:

https://www.dashingtweeds.co.uk/

Drink Well!

Drinking & Knowing Things
#47: VIN DOUX NATUREL

Now that you are all enormous Port aficionados, it's time to up your Port game. Any tool can wander into a wine store with a hundred bucks and come out with a decent Port that they can bring to a party and look cool. But you are part of the DAKT street crew, and we play the wine game at an entirely different level. Our goals are simple:

Have the best possible drinking experience at the lowest possible price.

Be the dopest Wineaux at every single party by bringing the wines that no one has heard of that blow peoples' minds.

Be the dopest Wineaux at every single fine dining experience by asking for shit that makes the somm run out from the back and want to talk to you, forcing all the beautiful people to ask "who the fuck is that and why is he/she getting all the attention?"

World Domination.

Because it's not just about Drinking Well, it's also about shoving our wine expertise down everyone else's throat. Literally. This isn't an ego play (well maybe just a little). It's more about trying to change the way Americans think and act about wine. In the US, people generally go after a small handful of the same old boring shit, which leaves so many amazing wines off the table.

Today we are gonna get geeky about alternatives to Port. Pay attention...

All over France, they make a style of wine they call Vin Doux Naturel (or naturally sweet wine). Feel free to think of these as French Port. But in true French style, they label each of these by the towns or areas where they are made. So there are like fifty different names you gotta know if you want to lean in on them, in marked contrast to the Portuguese who have their shit together on branding. The Portuguese decided to push the "Port" brand in the marketplace for all their stuff, where the French were like "no, our towns are special so we are gonna push the brand of each town".

Pro Tip: We call French Ports "VDNs" (for Vin Doux Naturel, of course).

Why VDNs are Dope AF:
Well, as with Port, the question ought to be "which VDNs are Dope AF?" There's as much sprawl with VDN styles and flavors as there is with Port. Except VDNs all have different names.

Production wise VDNs are similar to Port. Get the grapes fermenting, and then dump in brandy. Brandy kills the yeast and leaves the sugar, leaving a high alcohol wine (bonus!) which is also sweet.

And a similar wide range of grapes are allowed in VDN. White grapes, red grapes, and even gray (or gris) grapes are all allowed.

VDNs have a couple major differences from Port, however. The first is that the French are a bit more conservative with the brandy dump. Where Port usually ends up with 18-20% ABV, VDNs are usually 16-18%. And they often dump the brandy in later in the fermentation cycle, so the wines aren't quite as sweet (as more of the sugar has been eaten up by the yeast). So if you are one of those sanctimonious pricks who complains that Port is too big and sweet for you (no judgment, Paul), you might enjoy a VDN which has the volume turned down a bit on both of those dimensions.

The second major difference is with the aging. Port generally goes straight into a barrel, and then the only question is when to pull it out. Early is Ruby or Vintage, later is LBV and much later is Tawny. VDNs on the other hand are all over the map. Some people age it in tank, others in barrel, and some age it in big glass jars called "bonbonnes" that they put out into the sun and let cook like Grandma's old Lipton sun tea for years.

What this means is that it's hard to describe a "typical" style of VDN. Some are fruity and fresh while others are oxidized and nutty. Not to fear though – we have some simple rules for these as well.

The first style we are going to look for comes from the town of Banyuls and will be labeled "Banyuls". Banyuls is unique among the VDNs as they are the only place that designates some of the wine as Grand Cru (although these are a bitch to come by in the US). Grand Cru Banyuls is going to be dark berry flavors and rich full mouthfeel, similar to a Vintage Port, but you can generally find them for $20-30.

The second style we are going to look for is the "ambre" or brown styles. These are going to be very similar in style and flavor to a Tawny Port, but unlike Tawny Ports they generally are not blends of different vintages. Just old wine from a single year. My general go-to for this style is Rivesaltes, and the wines will be labeled "Rivesaltes" or "Rivesaltes Ambre".

Pro Tip: It's pronounced Reeve-So. Not Riv-A-Salts.

+1 Pro Tip: There is also an appellation called Muscat de Rivesaltes and the wines will be labeled as such. This is NOT the same as Rivesaltes. These wines are made from the Muscat grape and are not as good (IMHO).

Side Note: One of the best wine tasting notes I have ever heard was when Cristo and I were drinking a 1945 Rivesaltes. He put his nose in the glass and exclaimed "goddamn, this smells like the inside of an old Rolls Royce".

+1 Side Note: He was spot on.

And as with Port there are a whole boatload of other options, from fruit-driven styles from Rivesaltes, or from places like Maury or Rasteau. Don't worry about all these. Our simple VDN rules:

If it is white or pink, don't drink it.

If we want fruity red, we prefer Banyuls Grand Cru.

If we want caramel and dried fruit, look for Rivesaltes, and preferably one with as much age on it as you can find.

If you are curious and open to whatever is in the bottle just buy anything labeled VDN and give it a go. Just be prepared to not love all of them (but you can find them all day for under $25 so not a huge risk).

On to our recommendations. Now, I said that Banyuls Grand Cru was a bitch to find and as usual I was right. You don't become the World's Leading Wine Influencer by happenstance. I couldn't find much for sale online in the US (although to be honest I only spent about four minutes looking – you monkeys all know how to use Google). I did find a bunch in France for like $20 a bottle, but wasn't willing to spend a fortune on shipping. Anyway, here's an option.

Etoile Banyuls Grand Cru

For Rivesaltes I had an equally tough time but here's an option with some older vintages available for pretty cheap.

Arnaud de Villeneuve Rivesaltes Ambre

Drink Well!

Drinking & Knowing Things
#48: FOOD PAIRING

One of the longest running discussions in the world of wine is which wine to pair with which food. If you nail the pairing, it's pretty easy to see why this is a big deal. When you get it right it makes both the food and the wine better. Sometimes these experiences are borderline magical.

So everyone has opinions on how to do this right. In fact, this is a major reason why we even have sommeliers in the first place – so they can tell us what we should be drinking with our meals. Unfortunately, this breaks down all the time because:

a. People think they know what they want so they order the same old Caymus with whatever food they are having.
b. Somms are often trying to move weight, so there's an incentive for them to go with the highest price option rather than the perfect option.
c. Lastly, and most importantly – everyone's tastes and preferences are different. Some people are more sensitive to sour, or sweet. Or some people are allergic to tannin. Whatever. The point is that even the "perfect" pairing might not be perfect for you. You all know my thoughts on the goddawful port and chocolate pairing that morons seem to love.

Bottom line is that you are going to have to experiment a bit to find out what works for you. I'm gonna give you some tips, and then am going to share the results of a recent experiment that I did.

Side Note: I'm writing this intro in advance of actually doing the experiment so I have no fucking idea if it is going to work out or not. But I'm gonna share the results regardless.

How to Create Dope AF Pairings:

First Tip, and probably the easiest one to remember: If it grows together it goes together. (As long as it's European.) The strategy is that wherever they have been making food and wine in the same place for hundreds of years they have them pretty dialed in together, e.g. Chianti goes with pasta. But this is a fairly pedestrian approach.

Second Tip: Acid cuts fat. Any wine with high acidity is gonna pair great with any fatty dish. This is why we see white wine cream sauces on pasta. Or why Sauternes and foie gras go well together (Sauternes has elevated acid, even though you don't really notice it because the wine is so sweet).

Third Tip: Tannins attach themselves to protein. One of the reasons why you feel them in your cheeks. Because you are made of protein (delicious human protein). Also why Cab goes well with steak.

Fourth Tip (and for me probably the most important): The power of the wine ought to match the power of the food. You want them to complement each other, not have one completely overshadow the other. Power is a bit of an elusive concept, but the way I think about it is sort of a combination of the body, mouthfeel, texture and concentration of the wine. You wouldn't want to have a huge Bordeaux with a salad, but it is gonna go goddamn great with some big meaty lamb chops. It's a bit esoteric, particularly with dishes that have some complexity of flavor and texture.

But this whole thing should be fun, not intimidating, so don't forget Wine Etiquette Rule #1 which is "There Are No Rules". Do whatever you want and drink whatever you like.

Side Note: We used to run a recurring sequence on RockNRoll Wine School which tried different wines with foods like bacon or fresh baked chocolate chip cookies. It was always super interesting to see what the crowd pleasers were, and they weren't always what you anticipated. For example we paired wines with an In-N-Out Double Double (which is the best hamburger in the world btw, despite what the idiots on the East Coast keep saying about that crappy Steak Shack place which competes with In-N-Out in the same way that Arby's competes with Mortons), and the unanimous favorite was a slightly off dry Riesling.

I thought I would put my wine pairing skills to the test with a food that I don't know shit about – which is caviar. My friend and DAKT Street Team member Jennifer is a caviar broker. (I know, right – who the hell gets to be a caviar broker? I feel like Bender in Breakfast Club. "Carl, how does one *become* a caviar broker? Brian here is interested in the ichthyological arts....)

Anyway, Jennifer convinced me that I needed to up my caviar game. She was thoughtful enough to provide both knowledge and caviar from Black River Caviar for me to run this little experiment. I'll walk you through my thought process and then let you know how it worked out.

Some background on caviar. Apparently it's complicated, and there's a bunch of garbage out there labeled caviar but really isn't. That said, I assume that caviar is going to be rich in mouthfeel and flavor, as well as having some good salinity. Generally caviar is going to be about 58% fat, 36% protein and 6% carbs. So it's keto AF as well, albeit perhaps not the most price savvy keto diet addition.

Side Note: I looked those percentages up on the internet, so they are as accurate as anything one finds on the internet.

My thought process was as follows:

Caviar's high in fat, so I want a wine with high acidity. But perhaps also some tannin because of the protein. Whatever wine I pick is going to need to have some body and power to stand up to the power of the caviar but not overpower it. Also, I wasn't willing to drive over to my wine storage facility because we are on lock down, and more importantly I am a lazy piece of shit, so I was fettered by whatever inventory I had in the home cellar.

Given these factors, I concluded I was going to try the following:

1. A 2015 Barolo. High in both acid and tannin. Hopefully big enough to stand up to how flavorful I believe the caviar is going to be. Might be a bit young but fuck it.

2. I want something super high in acid. I considered both Chenin Blanc and Riesling, since I know both of those are high in acid and both are great food wines. But I ended on a Vintage Champagne. Very high in acid, but with some rich body from the extended aging on lees. (Also I know that Champagne is a traditional pairing with caviar, so I'm cheating a bit.) Caveat: turns out I didn't have any Vintage Champagne in the home cellar but I did have a 2010 Blanc de Blanc with seven years lees aging from Alta Langa so I went with that.

3. Some of the flavor notes indicated that one of the caviars (Jennifer sent me three different ones) was going to be nutty and flavorful so I want something that is oxidized to get that nutty complement. I considered Madeira or Manzanilla Sherry but I think they are going to be too big of a wine. So I am going with a 2015 CUNE Monopole Classico, which is an amazing white Rioja, so it will be oxidized, but also happens to have a bit of Manzanilla mixed in (this is a spectacular wine for $25 btw – make sure you get the Classico version which has the Manzanilla mixed in). Vin Jaune was also a strong contender here, but I had to make a game time decision.

4. A Provence Rosé. This one is a bit of a wild card, but I want to see what happens. I think it might be too light.

5. And since I was just writing about Sauternes I grabbed a 2009. We'll see.

The Results:
Ok, so I should probably describe the caviars. As mentioned, I had three different ones.

- The Imperial was light in color but full bodied and super savory.
- The Royale was dark and rich and creamy
- The Tradition was super well balanced between savory and salty and was really accessible. For the record, this one was my favorite caviar. It's probably because it wasn't as bold as the other two and I am a caviar rookie.

Side Note: The tasting notes that came with the caviar included a wine pairing suggestion for each. Each was paired with Vintage Champagne. Pussies....

Now, what happened:

- As expected, the Vintage Blanc de Blanc worked extremely well with all three. But nothing about it made me stick my head up and bellow "Fuck Yeah!!" like Mel Gibson screaming "Freeeedommmm" at the end of Braveheart. It was functionally great but nothing magical. Like the Acura NSX. Technically it's a super car, but not the kind that is gonna be noisy and spill oil all over your garage and viscerally involve you in the experience and piss off Ann. Great, but lacking in the quality of "being interesting".

- The Rosé was fucking terrible across the board. Don't do this. Just awful.

- I had high hopes for the white Rioja. Although I love that Monopole Classico, I was a bit disappointed with how it performed with the caviar. It was too savory for the Imperial and overpowered it. It worked OK with the other two but once again nothing too special. Which means a Vin Jaune or a Sherry would have likely been worse because they are even more savory.

- The Barolo was outstanding. I was a bit worried because drinking a 2015 Barolo breaks my rule of waiting at least seven years to drink a Barolo. I was nervous it would be too tight. But it worked fantastically with all three. It was exactly the right level of power, and blended seamlessly with all of them.

- The Sauternes: Holy. Fucking. Shit. This was amazing. With all three, the first sip of the Sauternes overpowered the caviar. But after about two seconds, the caviar stepped up (or maybe the Sauternes stepped down) and the two complemented each other perfectly, with a finish that lasted a couple of minutes and had this amazing blend of salinity and sweetness that was awesome.

Side Note: I forced Ann (who is not a caviar aficionado) to play this game with me. Her conclusions were almost identical to mine.

Which means I have done a phenomenal job of training her.

No, in fact her palate is better than mine, so the fact that she came to the same conclusions that I did means that they are probably pretty solid conclusions. And when we finished the whole experiment we chilled out and macked down all the rest of the caviar with pretty much all the rest of the Sauternes and ignored the other options, so that is the deciding factor. Without any specific objectives, the wine you naturally gravitate towards is the one that wins.

So what have we learned?

1. The analysis of acid/tannin/fat/protein will work pretty much always. You'll get something that's not gonna suck and embarrass you in front of your friends by picking a horrible pairing.
2. Sometimes the best pairings may not be the most obvious.
3. Taking the safe road and always picking the "traditional" pairing means you miss out on the big home runs. Chance favors the bold!

Also, caviar is way more interesting than I had previously thought. Big ups to Jennifer for forcing me to give this a deeper dive. And those of you who want to get in on this I would urge you to check out www. blackrivercaviar.com or give her a shout at jennifer.chin@brcaviar.com. Because she's a fucking caviar broker.

Normally I'd end with some wine recommendations, but not today. Today your homework is to try to look at what's for dinner and make a more informed pairing decision and see what happens. If by chance caviar is on the menu I'd strongly encourage you to forgo the Rosé.

Drink Well!

DRINKING & KNOWING THINGS
#49: GRENACHE

It seems like every hipster winemaker is jumping on the GSM bandwagon these days and bragging about it. It's like the Bitcoin of wine. I get it. It's made with a blend of Grenache, Syrah and Mourvèdre (generally speaking). All of these grapes have fairly high yields, so you can make more volume than other varietals on the same acreage. Since it's a blend, you're not locked into any specific profile. You can switch up the percentages in the blend to correct mistakes in the vineyard or the winery. Most people are familiar with the GSM blend branding, so it's easy to sell. And when it's done right, it's damn tasty to drink.

So a bunch of people are making a GSM blend. And frankly some of them are fucking it up. But that's not the point of this DAKT. The point of this is that if a blend of GSM can be dope, then what about the individual grapes that make up the GSM blend?

Well, we know that Syrah can be Dope AF. Refer to DAKT 30 on Cornas. And we know that Mourvèdre can also be Dope AF, from DAKT 19 on Bandol. Today we are gonna put the last piece of that puzzle together and talk about Grenache.

Why Grenache is Dope AF:
In my opinion, people either "get" Grenache or they don't. The small percentage of folks who get it are borderline maniacal about it, where the vast majority who don't get it are like Grenache, yeah, whatever. Here's why I think many people aren't super excited about it: Grenache is the most widely planted red grape in the world.

Side note: I'm not sure if that statistic is true today, or if it refers to production of volume or the most acres under vine. And I'm too lazy to look it up. But I know at one point it was the biggest by some metric. Doesn't matter – the point is that there is a fuckload of Grenache made around the world.

Grenache is widely planted because it is fairly easy to grow, adapts to most soils and weather, has a strong trunk and good yields. It also ripens way later than everything else so you can stage production if you have limited production capacity (e.g. make the Cab first and then get it out of the tanks before you harvest the Grenache). All these factors make it a reasonable choice for farmers to grow.

Side Note: Grenache was one of the first European varieties planted in California in the 1800s.

The problem is that Grenache lacks color, acid and tannins. It's like the Coke Zero of red wine. So on its own it generally isn't that much fun. But you can blend it in with other stuff, provide some fruitiness to the blend and increase the volumes. Which is what most people do.

However!

If you reduce yields of Grenache, generally by cropping back the fruit, then magically Grenache gets more phenolically ripe. Which is a fancy wine geek term for now it has more color, tannins, and acid.

This is what they do in the high-dollar areas of the Rhône, like Châteauneuf du Pape. But we don't want to pay high CDP prices to get kickass single-variety Grenache. Consequently in this case we must look towards Spain.

In Spain, they call the grape Garnacha, and it's grown all over the place. In most places it's used as the workhorse grape. They keep those yields high and produce rather uninteresting single variety wines and have a bunch of volume left over to blend in with other wines. But over the last couple of decades people have figured this shit out and are starting to hold yields back in order to produce a much higher quality Garnacha.

While this approach is beginning to be embraced by producers all over, there are big concentrations in a couple of regions. One is Priorat. I am kind of iffy on Priorat. This region somehow became the press darling of the wine world maybe ten or fifteen years ago and people are all over the goddamn moon about it. While I think the wines from there are solid, in my experience they are:

a. Often faulted or dirty
b. Way more pricey than they should be (IMHO)

But maybe I think that they're more pricey than they should be because there is another area to get great Garnacha that is not very well known, so there isn't the price premium of Priorat.

"Stop dick teasing us already Mike and tell us what it is!"

I'm getting there. This is my process. I gotta lead you along so that by now you are salivating all down your chin and getting antsy and also pissed at me for taking so long to get to the goddamn point.

That's how you know my "writing device" is working.

I'm still doing it right now, aren't I?

It's fucking annoying, isn't it?

Ok, I'll stop doing that and tell you.

Side Note: sometimes I put a side note to break up the flow and force you to wait a little while longer.

Pro Tip: sometimes I do this with pro tips as well.

I am seriously dying laughing right now. But I'll cut to the chase. The answer is Campo de Borja and the wines will be labeled as such.

Campo de Borja has pretty much the same legal requirements as Rioja, if you remember those from DAKT 24. The youngest are called Crianza (aged for twenty-four months). Then there is Reserva (aged for thirty-six months, with a minimum of twelve in barrel). Lastly there is Gran Reserva (aged for sixty months with a minimum of twenty-four in barrel). As with Rioja, the good producers exceed these limits, sometimes by a considerable margin. These represent some of the greatest values in aged red wines on the planet.

So get after it already. Caveat – avoid anything under $15 from Campo de Borja or anything that isn't Garnacha. If it's single varietal Garnacha and over $15 you should be getting some of the primo stuff.

<u>Bodegas Morca Godina Campo de Borja</u>

As always, Drink Well!!

DRINKING & KNOWING THINGS
#50: AGIORGITIKO

We've been making wine for a damn long time. Depending on who you ask, we believe winemaking has been around for six thousand years or so. To put it in context, this is a couple of thousand years before we have any record of written languages. So when Mrs. England, my high school English teacher, admonished me for not taking English seriously and preferring to go out and party instead, she was ignoring the demonstrable fact that partying had been prioritized ahead of writing for millennia before Jesus. (Who burst on to the scene by guess what? Making wine.)

Clearly I am an old soul.

Up until about maybe forty or so years ago, everyone made wine the same way. Pick some grapes, smash 'em up, let them sit around and eventually fermentation will start. Let the fermentation run its course, strain out the big chunks and put the liquid into some kind of vessel to store it in.

This worked, but it wasn't really the best way to do it. We didn't know about microorganisms, or filtration methods, or how to manage fermentations, or sterilization, or how yeast worked. We didn't have labs or sensors, or temperature controls. We ended up with wine, but a lot of it was bad, and we had to throw herbs in it, or cook it, or dump brandy into it so it wouldn't go bad or make people sick or die.

Technology got better, and winemakers and scientists started to figure this shit out, and over time wine got better. The last forty years or so in particular has seen winemaking and wine quality increase by ridiculous orders of magnitude.

Side Note: Some purists reject that these methods have made wine better, and prefer to make "natural wine" by doing things the old way. These people are complete idiots, and the vast majority of natural wine is fucking disgusting.

+1 Side Note: I have had some natural wines (maybe 5% of them) which are delicious, but this is always a function of a very experienced winemaker who knows what they are doing and can manage the process effectively. I guess it is like an experienced baker carefully making artisanal bread without preservatives, versus my kids slapping some flour and water together and calling the resulting runny mess "focaccia". Most of the natural wine out there falls into the latter category, more's the pity.

Anyway, what we see is that in some of the old school wine regions where they have been making wine for thousands of years these newer techniques are just starting to come into play. As the archaic methods are being replaced by science and technology, without fail they are transforming the local wine scene and we are seeing quantum leaps in the quality of the wine. Greece is no exception, and that is why this is the third Greek wine I've talked about in the fifty-two DAKTs so far. Suffice it to say that I am pretty stoked about what's going on down there.

Side Note: It doesn't hurt that the Greek economy is in the toilet right now so wines from there also represent incredible bargains.

+1 Side Note: The market works however, and so this financial incentive will eventually diminish. Refer to the DAKT on Portugal if you need a reminder.

Why Agiorgitiko is Dope AF:
All Greek wines need a pronunciation guide; in this case "Ah-Your-Yee-Tee-Ko". Which is fun to throw around e.g. "Yo, you wanna pop open this Agiorgitiko?".

Agiorgitiko is a red wine, primarily grown in Nemea, which is in the Peloponnese region on the mainland northwest of Athens. The wines are full-bodied and fruity, with elevated tannins that are soft in character. In the better wines, you'll also get spicy undertones. They kind of remind me of bolder versions of Mencia or Grenache.

Unfortunately, as with both of those other grapes, there's a more moderate version of Agiorgitiko which is nothing special, other than being cheap. Also we have to factor in that modernization is occurring in Nemea heterogeneously, which is a fancy way of saying that not everyone is doing it. There's a high degree of standard deviation on the quality metric there.

But the good ones can be amazing. I once spent a day at Ieropoulos Family winery there, where the owner (who is perhaps the most intense winery owner I have ever met) is convinced that Agiorgitiko can rival Burgundy. While I don't know that as of today I fully agree with that statement, I applaud his energy and optimism. They're making small batch Agiorgitiko in a Burgundian style, and his wines are off the chain delicious.

Side Note: He was aging his wine in French Oak barrels until he decides it's ready for prime time. At the time I was there, he had been aging stuff for four years and still was sitting on it because he didn't think it was quite ready yet. I kept an eye out for it here in the US and after a couple of years eventually saw it on the list at Milos at the Cosmopolitan in Vegas. I ordered some and the sommelier literally shit his pants that I knew what it was and wanted some. It was even better two years later.

So I am super excited about what may come out of Nemea over the next few years. We're still in early days, but a number of the larger wineries there are investing a ton of cash on modernization, and I think it's only one Wine Spectator story from getting blown up. I'd be a little worried that as the World's Leading Wine Influencer I might spur this on, but I know that all you DAKT Street Team members know enough to keep your mouths shut on the secret stuff, and won't go blabbing to all your friends about it.

Now, our recommendations. Given the nascent state of development here, we're definitely going to use a price rule for Agiorgitiko. The old school guys don't have any capital expenditures to recoup, so they're all going to be selling their stuff for probably under $12. We're going to want to stay above probably $16 in order to get something decent.

Good luck finding the Ieropoulos Family. I did a global search on Wine Searcher and found one place that was selling it retail (in New York, oddly enough). Too bad suckers; I bought their entire stock (which was only four bottles, but I'll take it).

But we have other decent options. I'm a big fan of Gaia. Grab some of their Estate wine for $20 a bottle.

Gaia Estate Red

Drink Well!

Drinking & Knowing Things
#51: SAUTERNES

When I first started writing these wine recommendations a year ago, I had no idea that DAKT would become the world-wide cultural phenomenon that it is today. I mean, I knew I was a fucking wine genius, but I had no idea that I was creating a whole movement and also a new word that would become part of the wine vernacular. Every day I get texts, emails and calls asking about DAKT this and DAKT that and how DAKT changed their life, and using DAKT as a noun, and an adjective, and a verb and probably an adverb too. It's crazy, but also speaks to the way in which we screwed up wine in this country by making it this whole intimidating and inaccessible thing. But we're changing all that and frankly I should be immediately canonized as the patron saint of Drinking Well. Feel free to start petitioning your local parish....

As we head into the Christmas week, I thought I would do something extra special to celebrate both DAKT and Christmas. Then I realized that every single DAKT is extra special, so I'm simply gonna do what I always do which is introduce you to something awesome and talk shit on Erik.

Today's shit talking is brought to you by Sauternes. Primarily because I'm still stoked about our recent food pairing experiment. It reminds me of what a Sauternes winemaker once said to me. "Sauternes is at its core a wine. Treat it like a wine."

Which means there are likely more use cases for Sauternes worth exploring then I am aware of.

Why Sauternes is Dope AF:
I think pretty much any botrytized wine is Dope AF. Despite how disgusting the process is, the output is amazing. For those of you who don't remember DAKT 23: Tokaji, a botrytized wine is a regular white

wine (Sauvignon Blanc and/or Semillon in Sauternes' case) which has been infected with a fungus that rots the grapes and turns them black. The winery goes through and picks off the rotten berries which are shriveled up. Then they ferment this thick pasty mash and what comes out is this glorious sweet honeyed nectar of a wine. It's expensive because:

a. It's a labor-intensive process to pick individual grapes.
b. You lose most of your volume. They say that Château d'Yquem (the granddaddy of Sauternes) only gets one glass of wine per vine.
c. Apparently it also pairs amazingly well with caviar.

So Sauternes is a good thing. But the cost of it makes it less accessible. Not to worry. You all have the World's Leading Wine Influencer to show you how to hack the system.

Side Note: At one point a bottle of 1811 Château d'Yquem held the record for the most expensive bottle of wine ever sold.

Sauternes is a region in Bordeaux, a little bit south of where they make those big powerful red wines from Cabernet and Merlot. There's actually five villages that are allowed to produce this style of wine and label it as Sauternes. One of the villages is called Barsac. Barsac is unique because it is the only one of the five villages that has the option to label their wine as Barsac instead of Sauternes.

Why would anyone do this? Sauternes is the brand that has global recognition and also commands huge price premiums, where pretty much no one knows WTF a Barsac is. It sounds like an evil hobbit-menacing Tolkien character.

I have a theory on this. I think in France, many people make wine to sell wine, and they market it accordingly. But occasionally, there's a producer who is less motivated by money, and is more motivated by pride, or family honor because the vineyard has been in the family since Charlemagne, or because they are fanatical about wine, and they only produce a small quantity which they know they can sell 100% of every year locally so they don't give a shit about marketing to the rest of the world and trying to establish global distribution chains.

I like the fanatics! They're just hard to find if you're not a local or willing to drive around a bunch of tiny villages looking for them (which for the record I am totally willing to do). In the case of Barsac I can think of no other reason why someone would deliberately opt in to sell their product as a lesser known brand. This would be akin to Rolls Royce saying, fuck it, we're owned by Volkswagen so let's start badging up the Wraith with a VW emblem instead of that crappy old Spirit of Ecstasy hood ornament.

So if you see something labeled Barsac, odds are it's a Dope AF Sauternes made by a fanatical traditionalist. Buy these.

Right outside of Sauternes, there's a handful of other villages that produce the same style of wine. Since they're not part of the big five, they can only put the name of their village on the bottle. These are great options as well, and there's a number of them. I'm gonna make it easy and only talk about three.

Cadillac: Furthering our car analogy above, one town is called Cadillac. Literally it's the Cadillac of sweet Bordeaux wines.

Side Note: Cadillac was recently allowed to start producing red wines labeled Cadillac as well. So be careful to grab the white.

Loupiac: Another similar village.

Sainte-Croix-du-Mont: One of the harder names to remember, but same style.

All three of these are going to be high-quality botrytized wines, but will be way way cheaper than Sauternes. Now there are purists and snobs who will argue that the quality of wine from these villages is lower than Sauternes, and yeah, they're probably right, at least for the top Sauternes producers. But if d'Yquem or Rieussec was given an "A", these other wines would probably get an "A-" or a "B+" at the lowest. But instead of paying $400 a bottle, you can find these for $20 a bottle or less. From a value perspective, the trade off is totally worth it.

Barsac is relatively easy to get in the States, the other three not so much. But worth doing some digging to try to find them. If nothing else just so you can show up for Christmas dinner with a bottle of Cadillac under your arm and when your status-conscious sister-in-law asks what it is you can just smile knowingly.

Some recommendations: (FYI a lot of these wines are sold in half-bottles, so adjust accordingly. I usually prefer half-bottles because a full bottle of Sauternes is a bitch to get through without a few friends to help.)

A Barsac:

Château Coutet Barsac

A Cadillac:

Château Fayau Cadillac

And a St. Croix du Mont!

Château La Rame St Croix du Mont

Drink Well!

p.s. I totally forgot to talk shit on Erik. Sorry folks, next time...

DRINKING & KNOWING THINGS
#52: CRÉMANT

Ah, New Year's Eve. Time to slam the fucking door shut on this shitshow of a year and get back to some level of normalcy. Hopefully anyway. But before that, there's a New Year's Eve celebration to attend to. A socially distant, quarantined-at-home watching some bullshit virtual ball drop celebration, but a party nevertheless. And a NYE party demands bubbles.

And hence we are going to talk about bubbles. I know many of you remember DAKT 5 and 6 on Champagne, because people constantly text me photos of them enjoying their Champagne in the proper white wine glass instead of one of those goddawful flutes or coupes. Nice work, people. Keep it up.

But Champagne and other vintage alternatives to Champagne remain reasonably highly priced. What's a fella to do if he simply wants a nice, easy drinking bottle of bubbles, which is delicious but isn't going to break the bank if some asshole shakes it up and sprays it all over the place? The answer is simple: Crémant.

Side Note: Please take notice that I took the extra thirty seconds to find the little "e" with the notch over it to make the spelling of Crémant precise. You're Welcome...

Why Crémant is Dope AF:
Let's start by talking about what Crémant is. Crémant basically means "sparkling wine" in French. Sparkling wine made in the region of Champagne is called Champagne. Sparkling wine made everywhere else in France is called Crémant de XXXX, where XXXX is the name of the region. You'll see Crémant de Loire (from the Loire), Crémant de Alsace (from Alsace), Crémant de Borgogne (from Burgundy), Crémant de Jura

(from, yeah you guessed it, the Jura), and so on. However, most Crémant style wines differ from the revered Champagne wines in a couple of ways.

The first main difference is the level of bubbliness (or mousse, for you Wineauxs). The level of bubbliness in sparkling wines is measured in Atmospheric Pressure (or ATMs). The higher the pressure in the bottle, the more bubbles. The winemaker controls how much pressure is in the finished wine by deciding how much sugar they want to dump into the bottle before the second fermentation. More sugar means more food for the yeast, which then shit out more CO_2 which dissolves into the wine. Winemakers in Champagne aim for about six ATMs of pressure. Theoretically you could probably make a wine that had eight or ten ATMs if you could make the glass strong enough to hold it, but at six ATMs of pressure inside the bottle you are already at the risk of the bottle exploding, especially if it gets hot.

> **Side Note:** One time I accidentally left a bottle of Champagne in the front seat of my friend's Mercedes 380SL convertible in Las Vegas. When we got back to the car, it had exploded violently and the entire inside of the car was covered in glass fragments and hot sticky Champagne that had sat all day in one hundred twenty degrees and baked into the seats and the roof liner and basically everything.

> **+1 Side Note:** My friend was much less amused by this than I was.

Anyway, six ATMs is good for Champagne and that level of pressure is also what allows you to saber a bottle, which is where you hit the neck of the bottle with a special sword that weakens the glass and the cork and part of the neck pop off and it looks really fucking badass. Feel free to Google "Champagne Saber Video" and spend ten minutes being amused. (I can neither confirm nor deny my presence in any saber videos you find that look like me...)

But six ATMs is a lot of pressure. For Crémants made everywhere else in France the winemakers aim for about four ATMs instead of six. This makes Crémants much less bubbly (and also harder to saber). So they are easier to pound. It's slightly fizzy, instead of being super powerfully fizzy.

The second major difference is the length of aging on lees. The rule for basic Champagne is eighteen months on lees in the bottle, and for Vintage Champagne it is three years. And many of the higher end Champagnes age for much longer than that. Crémant, in contrast, only is required to age on lees for nine months (although the specific rules for production vary in different regions). Some producers will age it a bit longer, but generally speaking the producers know that if you want those deep bready yeasty flavors that come from extended aging on lees that you're gonna buy Champagne, so they don't incur the extra time and inventory carrying costs to age it longer.

What this means is that with Crémant you will get much less of the bready character and much more of the fruit character of the wine. Which again makes them super fresh and easy to drink.

The third major difference is the grapes. In Champagne, production is limited to Pinot Noir, Chardonnay, and/or Munier. In Crémant, it's made from whatever grapes they grow in that local region. In the Loire you will get Crémant made from Chenin Blanc, or in Alsace from Pinot Blanc, or in Bordeaux from Sauvignon Blanc. Which means there is way more variability in flavor profiles. Champagne has a specific style – high acidity, high bubbles, and high yeasty character. The only difference is the quality of the grapes and the aging levels. But Crémant is all over the place.

The fourth difference, and the best difference of all is the price. Most Crémant wines are under $20. You wanna ball out and drop $25 and you are getting the best of the best. That same $25 barely gets you into the lowest and shittiest Champagnes.

So done deal, I am all in on Crémant. I love Vintage Champagne, but for everyday bubbles drinking I drink Crémant. I bet my consumption of Crémant is ten times my consumption of Champagne. And I do have some favorites. My main go-tos are Crémant de Alsace and Crémant de Loire. I especially love the rosés from both of these places, which are made with Pinot Noir. And Crémant de Loire usually makes their white Crémants with Chenin Blanc, which as you all know is a grape I am a huge fan of as well.

I'd put a link in here with a recommendation but it's way too late to get anything delivered by tonight, unless you have Drizly in your area. But if you're running out to the liquor store last minute take a look at the bubbly section and grab anything that says Crémant on it and give it a go.

Drink Well!

WRAPPING UP

Well, that's it. Your masterclass is now complete. You all get an A (except Erik, who gets a D-minus). You now can both Drink and Know Things.

Hopefully you all had a lot of fun with this, learned a lot, drank some kickass stuff and some other stuff you hated and laughed your asses off. More importantly, my hope for all of you is that you:

a. Began to appreciate how broad and exciting the world of wine is.
b. Started dialing in your palates on what you like and don't like, and why. (Remember that this will continue to evolve so don't get complacent.)
c. Became more comfortable talking about wine with people and increased your confidence level when talking about wine.
d. Began trusting your opinions, no matter what the "experts" tell you what to think about specific wines.
e. Became the most exciting go-to wine person in your social group.
f. Became Dope AF.

What's next?
Well, that's up to you. I've been doing this for many years and I still don't see any end in sight. There's too much to know, do and experience. I think it is the journey that matters. The people you meet along the way and the experiences you have. Wine has a way of opening doors and creating connections between us, which at the end of the day matters a whole lot more than whatever bullshit possessions you accumulate over the small amount of time we get here.

So keep after it. Remember that you now have the wine chops to go toe-to-toe with most people you are going to encounter, and the super geeky ones will embrace you as one of your own. Time to take the red pill and see how deep the rabbit hole goes....

If you're getting passionate about it, feel free to go to www.drinkingandknowingthings.com and sign up for my weekly newsletter so you can keep getting new DAKTs on a weekly (ish) basis.

Lovers and haters can reach me at mike@drinkingandknowingthings.com.

Drink Well!

Made in United States
Troutdale, OR
10/12/2023

13604338R00126